JOINT STRIKE FIGHTER
Boeing X-32 vs Lockheed Martin X-35

Bill Sweetman

MBI Publishing Company

First published in 1999 by MBI Publishing Company, 729 Prospect Avenue, PO Box 1, Osceola, WI 54020-0001 USA

MBI Publishing Company books are also available at discounts in bulk quantity for industrial or sales-promotional use. For details write to Special Sales Manager at Motorbooks International Wholesalers & Distributors, 729 Prospect Avenue, PO Box 1, Osceola, WI 54020-0001 USA.

Library of Congress Cataloging-in-Publication Data Available

ISBN 0-7603-0628-1

On the front cover: The new swept-wing version of the Boeing JSF retains the basic construction of the original, with a thick one-piece wing and a straight-sided fuselage beneath it. A lighter, raked-back inlet has replaced the characteristic yawning-hippo inlet of the X-32. The small horizontal tails improve both pitch and roll control, because more of the trailing-edge surface can now be used to provide roll authority. *Boeing*

On the back cover: Full-scale mock-up of the USAF version of Lockheed Martin's JSF design, completed in 1998. The family resemblance to the F-22 is clear, with a sharp chine line along the fuselage. The weapons bay doors are visible forward of the main landing gear, which retracts forward into the wing-body junction: this means that the Navy fighter's heavier landing gear can be accommodated without changing the primary structure. *Lockheed Martin*

On the frontispiece: Simulation is an extremely important tool in JSF development. High-speed communications have made it possible to interlink simulators and other computers, and their users, across the US in real time. The "pilot" in this simulation, wearing a helmet-mounted display and using large-format color cockpit displays, could be taking part in a campaign-level simulation involving large friendly and hostile forces. *McDonnell Douglas*

On the title page: The large canopy makes the JSF look smaller than it is: in fact, the single-engine fighter has more installed thrust than the twin-engined F/A-18. The canopy looks large because it has an unusually low sill line: the CV version meets Navy requirements for over-the-nose visibility, while the STOVL version must have good downwards-and-sideways visibility, for obstacle clearance in a vertical landing. *Lockheed Martin*

Designed by Steve Hendrickson

Printed in Hong Kong

Contents

STOVL Groundwork

Under guard in a secure hangar, the new full-scale mock-up is an impressive sight. It is a supersonic multirole fighter, technically comparable to the best in existence. Its single engine is the most powerful in the world. A multimode radar and the latest in navigation systems and cockpit displays will enable its single pilot to tackle targets in the air, on the land, and at sea. Uniquely, though, this fighter will be able to take off from a few hundred feet of runway and land in its own length, so it will replace both carrier-based and land-based fighters.

The latest Marine Corps development of the Harrier is the AV-8B Plus. Changes include the Raytheon APG-65 radar, a forward-looking infrared sensor in the bulge in front of the windshield, leading-edge root extension (LERX) surfaces to improve instantaneous turn rate, and added dispensers for infrared decoys and chaff above the aft fuselage. Most Marine Corps AV-8Bs are undergoing a major rebuild to bring them to this standard. McDonnell Douglas

The engineers admire their creation before they leave for the weekend. A few of them stop for a drink, play some darts, and talk. The world is changing, and a man has to wonder where it will end. The kids dress strangely and want the latest gadgets—even record players and transistor radios, so that they can listen to the cacophonous noise of so-called musical groups with nonsensical names like the Beatles or the Rolling Stones.

It is 1964 in Kingston-upon-Thames, England. The Hawker Siddeley P.1154 fighter is within a few months of being scrapped by a new Labour Party government. By the time another supersonic short take-off and vertical landing (STOVL) fighter is ready to fly in the West, the Stones and Beatles will be Classic Rock, and the designers' kids will be resisting demands from their own children for Nintendo 64 and DVD movie players, devices that make the P.1154's navigation gear look like something from the Flintstones.

If there is a more tortuous tale in the history of aerospace than the long pursuit of a runway-free fighter, the author has not heard it. Of all the twists and reverses in this story, the latest is the most remarkable. Once almost given up for dead, STOVL has become the driving requirement behind the Joint Strike Fighter (JSF), which its planners expect to be the largest fighter program in history.

To understand where JSF is going, it is necessary to know something of how it came to be here in the first place. The roots of the story go back beyond Surrey in the 1960s, to Paris in the 1950s.

The first attempts at building a vertical take-off and landing (VTOL) fighter involved small airplanes, large engines, and an unusual take-off attitude. The Ryan X-13 Vertijet tail-sitter was the most successful of three such aircraft tested in the United States. It even landed and took off in the Pentagon parking lot. Foreshadowing the strong U.S.–U.K. collaboration in this area, it had a Rolls-Royce Avon engine. Bill Sweetman

U.S. Air Force Colonel Willis Chapman had commanded a B-25 group in Italy in 1944–45 (one of his bombardiers was a would-be writer named Joseph Heller) and later headed the first U.S. Air Force jet bomber group, flying B-45 Tornadoes. In 1956, he was sent to Paris as the U.S. Air Force representative for the Pentagon's Mutual Weapons Development Plan (MWDP) field office. The objective of the MWDP was to find and support innovative ideas in Europe's defense

The Harrier GR.1 made its first flight in 1966. Although it looked like the earlier P.1127 and Kestrel, it was heavier, more powerful, and almost entirely redesigned in detail, with elements of the P.1154 avionics. Later, the RAF GR.1s were updated into GR.3s, with a laser seeker in the nose. British Aerospace

The supersonic P.1154, seen here in a two-seat version for the Royal Navy, resembled a larger, more slender P.1127. It was powered by the BS.100 engine, with plenum-chamber burning (PCB)—a system that burned fuel in the fan nozzles, boosting thrust, and jet velocity. Its cancellation was not an unmixed curse; investigations showed that development would have been difficult. British Aerospace

industry so that it could make a stronger contribution to NATO.

Bill Chapman had not been in Paris long when French designer Michel Wibault approached his office with a design for a vertical take-off fighter. It had a turboprop engine, driving four centrifugal "snail" fans on the

Germany's EWR VJ101C, with its wingtip-mounted pairs of tilting engines, hovers in a rig and demonstrates why the use of augmented thrust in vertical mode is no simple matter. The VJ101 was inspired by work done at Bell and Ryan and combined lift-cruise engines at the wingtips with lift-only engines behind the cockpit. The principal limitation was that the tip pods could not be rotated quickly enough for a Harrier-type short takeoff. DaimlerChrysler Aerospace

sides of the fuselage. The fans could swivel through 90 degrees to point their exhausts downward for take-off or aft for level flight.

Chapman was familiar with contemporary attempts to build VTOL fighters. Lockheed and Convair had built two extraordinary fighter prototypes for the U.S. Navy. Fitted with enormous propellers, they stood on their tails for take-off and landing, so that the pilot was on his back with his feet in the air. ("A good position," said one pilot, "but not for flying.") Other companies were working on "flat-risers"—some with batteries of small jet engines that were used only for vertical lift and others with swiveling engines. Wibault's idea was different, Chapman thought, and worthy of further investigation.

The U.S. Air Force officer showed the Wibault design to Dr. Stanley Hooker, technical director of the Bristol Aero Engine Company. MWDP had funded Bristol's Orpheus jet engine. Assigned by Hooker to look at the concept, engineer Gordon Lewis was impressed by Wibault's idea of deflecting the airflow and thrust, rather than rotating the airplane or the engine. Lewis designed a simpler engine, which used the first two stages of Bristol's Olympus jet engine as a fixed, axial fan, with rotating nozzles to deflect the exhaust.

A brochure on the resulting BE.53 engine reached Hawker Aircraft at Kingston in June 1957. Chief designer Sir Sydney Camm directed designer Ralph Hooper to explore its potential. Hooper saw that he needed all the vertical thrust that the engine could provide in order to produce a workable aircraft. The BE.53 evolved into a turbofan with four rotating nozzles, one pair deflecting the fan stream and another for the core exhaust. When Chapman visited the Hawker hospitality chalet at the Farnborough air show in September 1957, Hooper and Camm showed him a preliminary design for the P.1127, a small fighter with the BE.53 engine and a shoulder-mounted wing.

By May 1958, MWDP funding had been found for the BE.53 engine, now named Pegasus.

The VJ101C's operational follow-on was canceled, leaving the subsonic VAK 191B as the remaining German V/STOL fighter. Its Rolls-Royce RB.193 engine had four rotating nozzles, like the Harrier's Pegasus, but the lift/cruise engine was smaller and was backed up by two RB.162 lift-jets. It was less flexible and more complicated than the Harrier and was abandoned after limited flight testing. DaimlerChrysler Aerospace

Funding the P.1127 proved more difficult because the British Ministry of Defence (MoD) had little interest in subsonic fighters. Hawker started building the first two prototypes on company funds, and the first aircraft was complete by the time the MoD agreed to support construction of six prototypes in August 1960. In the United States, NASA supported the program by building and testing small free-flight models. These demonstrated that, unlike most contemporary VTOL designs, the P.1127 could be flown without a complex autostabilization system. On October 21, 1960, the first P.1127 made its first wobbly hovering flights.

Early tests demonstrated the critical advantages of what Hawker and Bristol were now calling "vectored thrust." Unlike any other VTOL concept of the time, the P.1127 had one engine, no thrust blockers, and no diverter valves. The engine's flow path was constant from start to shutdown. Because the engine

Dassault adopted Rolls-Royce's V/STOL solution, using batteries of small jet engines for lift. The company's Mirage III-V had eight lightweight Rolls-Royce RB.162s buried in its midriff. The lift engines delivered 16 pounds of thrust for every pound of weight, but the space required for the engines, inlets, and exhausts drove up the air-plane's size and weight. Dassault

was fixed and the nozzles moved (courtesy of a Rube Goldberg arrangement of shafts and chains), the thrust vector could be moved quickly and precisely. This, the designers and test pilots found, meant that the aircraft could combine jet and wing lift for a very short take-off, lifting a much greater useful load than was possible in a vertical departure.

As prototype testing continued, the Royal Air Force prepared a draft operational require-ment, OR345, for a V/STOL fighter based on the P.1127 design. V/STOL, however, was becoming the hot item within NATO, as the "nuclear trip-wire" strategy of the 1950s gave way to "flexible response." Tactical air power would be vital in containing a conventional Soviet attack, but long runways were targets for aircraft and missiles.

In 1961, NATO Basic Military Require-ment 3 (NBMR-3) defined a joint specification for a supersonic V/STOL fighter-bomber. Its importance was symbolic, since there was no commitment from any NATO country to buy the winning aircraft, but it spurred the Royal Air Force to drop OR345 in favor of the more ambitious NATO concept.

Companies in France, Germany, the Nether-lands, and Italy proposed radical supersonic V/STOL fighters. The first two were the most serious contenders. Dassault, working with Rolls-Royce, took the lift-jet approach. A German con-sortium, EWR, flew the VJ 101, with four engines paired in wingtip nacelles.

Hawker and Bristol's P.1154 was declared the technical winner of NBMR-3, but no

NATO member put any money into it except for Britain, which selected it to replace the RAF's Hunters and the Royal Navy's Sea Vixen all-weather fighters. (In early 1963, one of the P.1127s became the first jet V/STOL aircraft to land on an aircraft carrier.)

Definition did not proceed smoothly. The Royal Navy wanted a twin-engined aircraft, so Hawker designed a P.1154 with two Rolls-Royce Speys and a complicated cross-ducting system. The Royal Navy wanted a larger radar dish and a two-man crew. In fact, what the Navy wanted was an F-4 Phantom, and that is what the Royal Navy received after the P.1154 was canceled in early 1965.

Fortunately, Hawker's eggs were not all in one basket. While the P.1154 was being designed, the United Kingdom, United States, and West Germany had funded nine improved P.1127s named Kestrel. The sponsoring U.S. service was the Army, which was interested in acquiring its own close air support (CAS) fighters. The Kestrels were tested successfully, demonstrating that it was practical to operate V/STOL fighters away from conventional bases. When the P.1154 was canceled, the United Kingdom's MoD ordered a further development of the Kestrel as an operational aircraft.

By the time the Harrier GR.1 entered service with the Royal Air Force in 1969, almost

The second Mirage III-V had different inlets and exhausts to increase thrust. The transition was slow, in part because of the high inertia of the airflow through the lift engines. An important lesson, embodied on the Lockheed Martin JSF, was that the lift engine thrust needed to be vectored aft for acceleration. Dassault

The Soviet Union developed the Yak-38 V/STOL fighter to operate from its first aircraft carriers. The ships were remarkable hybrids, designed to carry fighters, helicopters, and long-range cruise missiles. Like the VAK 191, the Yak-38 was a lift-plus-lift/cruise design. The two lift engines were installed behind the cockpit, and the lift/cruise engine had two aft nozzles. Bill Sweetman

every other V/STOL development in the world had fizzled out. Some could not lift themselves off the runway. Others could not make it through transition safely. Most had proven unreliable and dangerous even under test conditions. The U.S. Army, which had sponsored V/STOL projects from Lockheed and Ryan as well as supporting the Kestrel, had lost its roles-and-missions fight with the U.S. Air Force and was put out of the jet business.

In 1969, apart from the Harrier, the only surviving jet V/STOL programs were Germany's VAK 191 and the work that Yakovlev was doing for the Soviet Navy. Determined to

acquire its own shipboard fighters, the Soviet Navy was building carriers and a new V/STOL fighter, the Yak-36MP.

The Harrier was the only V/STOL fighter in production and soon became unique in another way—as the first non-U.S. jet fighter to be acquired in quantity by the U.S. forces. The U.S. Marine Corps first evaluated the Harrier in 1968. With remarkable speed, the Marines secured approval to buy 110 AV-8A Harriers, and an order was signed in 1970.

From its conception, therefore, the V/STOL fighter was a product of Anglo-American collaboration, including the early MWDP backing for the engine and the Army's support for the Kestrel. The Marine Corps would become the largest and most dedicated operator of the Harrier and would play a pivotal role in its development.

The Harrier was an impressive aircraft, but it had some inherent limitations. It carried no radar, so its air combat capability was limited. It also had a mean streak. Unusually, the P.1127, Kestrel, and Harrier made their way through flight tests, until 1968, without a single fatal accident; but the statistics started to change as service pilots faced the challenge of flying the new jet. The principal problem

In 1973, the U.S. Navy ordered Rockwell's XFV-12A as a prototype for a Mach 2.4 V/STOL fighter. The exhaust from the Pratt and Whitney F401 engine was ducted to hollow-section "ejector flaps" on the wing and canard. The thrust boost achieved by this means was much less than had been predicted, and the XFV-12A could not leave the ground. The XFV-12A's failure was a primary reason for the use of large-scale powered models in subsequent ASTOVL programs. Boeing archives

The Sea Harrier FRS.1 entered service in 1979 and restored the Royal Navy's fixed-wing air power, lost with the retirement of the carrier's Ark Royal and Eagle. It was a straightforward adaptation of the GR.1, with a raised cockpit and a radar. Its armament included the AIM-9 Sidewinder and the BAe Sea Eagle antishipping missile. British Aerospace

new aircraft and was inundated with ideas. Lockheed-California proposed a propeller-driven tail-sitter. Boeing and Northrop both designed jet tail-sitters. British Aerospace—formed in 1974 by the nationalization and merger of Hawker Siddeley and British Aircraft Corporation—teamed with McDonnell Douglas to propose both an improved subsonic Harrier and a supersonic version with plenum-chamber burning, a system that burned fuel in the front nozzles.

The Navy rejected designs based on proven technology and chose Rockwell to build the XFV-12A. For takeoff and landing, the exhaust from the XFV-12A's engine was ducted to "augmentor" flaps in the wings and in the oversized canard. By dragging free-stream air through the flaps and increasing the mass flow, the augmentor flaps would boost the engine's thrust by 70 percent—in theory. John Fozard could not resist pointing out that the P.1127, in its first tests, had been tethered down, while the only way that the XFV-12A's propulsion could be tested in free flight was to lift part of its weight with a crane.

The Rockwell fighter's performance (or its lack thereof) was academic. The Navy's nuclear and aviation communities detested the SCS, and, in the 1974 budget debate, their friends on Capitol Hill scuttled it. (The "nukes" and the aviators recognized their debt to the chairman of the Senate Armed Services Committee, and the seventh Nimitz-class carrier is named the John C. Stennis.) Zumwalt was defeated, and the experience inoculated the U.S. Navy against V/STOL. Henceforth, anyone proposing a V/STOL fighter for the Navy was assumed to be a supporter of small, flimsy carriers.

The Royal Navy had lost its own large carriers—and its F-4s—as a consequence of defense cutbacks in the late 1960s. The Royal Navy was permitted to build three cruisers with full-length flight decks. Nominally built to carry large antisubmarine helicopters, the new ships were actually designed with V/STOL

was low-speed yawing, caused by the massive amounts of air flowing into the airplane ahead of the CG. The pilot who allowed the fighter to leave its safe flight envelope at low speed could quickly find his Harrier rolling out of control, often into a position where ejection was impossible.

As the Marines started to introduce the Harrier, the U.S. Navy flirted with V/STOL. When Admiral Elmo Zumwalt became chief of naval operations in 1970, the Navy could not see its way to replacing its aging Essex and Midway carriers with Nimitz-class supercarriers. From a study of alternatives, directed by Zumwalt, there emerged the Sea Control Ship, a mini-carrier equipped with supersonic V/STOL fighters and ASW aircraft.

In 1971, the Navy invited manufacturers to propose demonstration programs for the

in mind. After some delays, and in an atmosphere of austerity, the U.K. MoD approved development of the Sea Harrier FRS.1 in 1975.

After the U.S. Navy rejected the Harrier developments, BAe and McDonnell Douglas tried to interest the U.S. and British governments in the more powerful subsonic aircraft. Neither would fund it, but the U.S. Marine Corps sponsored a demonstration program, led by McDonnell Douglas, aimed at increasing the Harrier's range and payload at minimum cost. A new wing and other changes were tested on the YAV-8B, a modified AV-8A, starting in 1979. The Marine Corps decided to replace all its AV-8As and A-4 light-attack aircraft with a production version, the AV-8B Harrier II.

The Royal Air Force was still undecided about V/STOL in the late 1970s. Some factions in the Royal Air Force (RAF) looked at the Harrier's subsonic speed, its still-high accident rate, and the genuine logistical difficulties involved in off-base operations, and wondered whether the service should concentrate on conventional takeoff and landing (CTOL) fighters. On the other hand, there was concern about the ability of conventional air bases to survive attacks with concrete penetrators (like those the Israelis used to great effect in 1967), mines, or chemical weapons.

By this time, a change had entered the U.K. vocabulary. The term V/STOL gave way to STOVL (short takeoff, vertical landing). The change recognized the fact that Harriers in service invariably operated in STOVL mode, using 1,000 to 1,500 feet of road, taxiway, or other level surface to take off. STO boosted payload and range, and the runway requirement was still insignificant compared to a conventional fighter. Not only was the distance shorter, but the Harrier's low takeoff speed meant that it could tolerate rougher surfaces than a conventional jet.

In 1976, the MoD issued Air Staff Target (AST) 403, calling for an agile fighter with a good ground-attack capability. BAe's two

fighter divisions both produced designs to AST 403. The former BAC team at Warton designed a twin-engined CTOL fighter; the ex-Hawker Kingston group produced the P.1205, blending some distinctly F-16-like features with a four-nozzle PCB engine. In terms of performance, both aircraft were comparable.

Politically, P.1205 was a nonstarter. The Royal Air Force was traumatized by the cancellation of its key projects in the mid-1960s and knew that the Labour government of the 1970s would have axed the Tornado but for one factor: It was a multinational program and could not be scrapped without wrecking U.K.-German relations. Any new fighter, therefore, would be multinational, and in realistic terms this meant working with West Germany. The German defense ministry had backed a number of hopeless V/STOL fighter projects in the 1960s, and its view of STOVL was almost as jaundiced as that of the U.S. Navy.

The U.K. MoD consequently split its fighter requirement in early 1979. The AST 403 was to be a CTOL multinational aircraft and eventually led to the Eurofighter Typhoon. Air Staff Requirement (ASR) 409 was written around an improved Harrier; although Kingston proposed its own big-wing Harrier design, the MoD elected to join forces with McDonnell Douglas on the U.S. version.

The U.K.'s domestic STOVL efforts suffered another blow in that year when the British government announced plans to dispose of the Royal Navy's light aircraft carriers and Sea Harriers. But in April 1982, before these could be put into effect, Argentina seized the Falkland Islands.

To the Argentines' surprise, the British dispatched a task force to retake the islands, including the carriers Invincible and Hermes and 28 Sea Harriers. The Sea Harriers proved essential in blunting Argentine air attacks, shooting down 31 Argentine aircraft with no combat losses.

Ten Royal Air Force Harrier GR.3s were assigned to the force, but their departure was

17

delayed by training to deliver laser-guided bombs and modifications that allowed them to carry AIM-9 missiles. The first six aircraft were flown to Ascension Island, where they flew to the containership Atlantic Conveyor and landed on its deck. The ship followed the task force to the Falklands, where the Harriers flew to the Invincible and Hermes. The last four Royal Air Force Harriers to join the task force launched from Ascension and, with the help of Victor tankers, flew 4,000 miles into the South Atlantic, where, on a pitching deck in a war zone, their pilots made their first carrier landings.

Nine aircraft were lost in the campaign. Three of the Royal Air Force aircraft and two Sea Harriers were lost to ground fire. Early in the operation two Sea Harriers vanished in severe weather, probably as a result of a mid-air collision on patrol. One Sea Harrier slid off a carrier's deck while taking off in a Force 6 gale, and another crashed into the sea on takeoff.

Operations were carried out in weather that ranged from poor to appalling. There were four basic weather states, it was said later: fog, with 30-knot winds; clear weather, with 30-knot winds; gale conditions; and good weather, defined as sea state 4 or better. Conventional carrier-based aircraft cannot normally operate when the deck is pitching more than 6 to 7 degrees, but sea state did not affect Harrier operations at all, thanks to vertical landing. The Harriers landed opposite the island, where the pitching movement was smallest.

Look, Ma, no catapult! With a long history in CAS operations, the Marines saw air power differently from the Navy, which was responsible for developing Marine aircraft. Historically, the U.S. Marine Corps was concerned that the Navy's focus on deep-water operations and giant supercarriers would move their air support away from where it was needed. Here, an AV-8B takes off from the amphibious warfare ship USS Belleau Wood. McDonnell Douglas

The United States developed the AV-8B to improve the Harrier's payload and range. The key was a larger, thicker wing made from carbon-fiber composite material and a set of aerodynamic improvements, including strakes to capture the ground cushion beneath the aircraft and flaps that interacted with the aft nozzle flow to boost lift in STOL. The AV-8B was safer to fly than the AV-8A (with a new flight control system and more powerful roll nozzles) and with a war load and radius equal to conventional fighters. McDonnell Douglas

Fog did affect operations, and the aircraft sometimes had to find the carrier by its lights. One Sea Harrier was caught in fog and found the carrier on its second attempt with only 200 pounds of fuel left. The fog was so thick that the deck crew never knew the Harrier had landed.

Four accidental losses in 2,000 sorties is an impressive record for carrier operations. In wartime, with the aircraft operating well outside peacetime limits, it is quite remarkable. Considering that some of the crew had never been aboard a carrier before, it is astounding.

Reports of the Harrier's success soon reached Washington, and some people began to ask the U.S. Navy where its V/STOL plans had gone. Navy Secretary John Lehman retorted that the U.S. Navy would have been protected from air attack by its supercarriers and F-14s. He was right to a point, but at that time there was something he did not know, and few people know it now. At times in the Falklands, Sea Harriers flew when the cloud base was less than 100 feet above the ocean, and horizontal visibility was barely 250 yards (or the distance from Hermes' stern to her bow). Absolute minimum for U.S. Navy operations is a 200-foot ceiling and 880 yards of visibility.

By late 1982, the multinational Harrier program was healthy, with more than 400 AV-8Bs, GR.5s, and Sea Harriers on order. The Royal Navy's carriers had been reprieved, and the Navy was authorized to start a major upgrade program. The U.S. Marine Corps and Royal Navy were firmly committed to STOVL as the long-term solution to their air power requirements. The Spanish Navy had adopted the AV-8A in the mid-1970s, India acquired Sea Harriers in the mid-1980s, and Italy was building a new STOVL-capable carrier.

Ultimately, all these aircraft would need to be replaced, and it was this long-term

This is actually a good day in the South Atlantic: a mixed bag of Sea Harriers and RAF Harrier GR.3s on the carrier HMS Hermes during the Falklands War. The upward slope of the Ski-Jump ramp, developed under Royal Navy leadership, is visible at the left of the carrier's island. An inclined ramp on the bow of the ship, the Ski-Jump, was an aid to short takeoff, which converted some of the airplane's forward momentum into a vertical acceleration. This allowed it to complete its transition after a slower lift-off, and hence a shorter run. British Aerospace

Harriers flew more than 2,000 combat sorties over the Falklands, and on average more than 90 percent of the surviving aircraft were available for operations at any time. The main limitation was the availability of pilots rather than aircraft; the airplanes were averaging six to seven hours of flying time per day. On several occasions pilots were flying four one-hour combat sorties per day. Only 1 percent of missions were not completed. British Aerospace

requirement that would keep a flickering flame underneath the pot of advanced STOVL technology during most of the 1980s. Flickering, because the environment for STOVL was otherwise inhospitable. Anyone mentioning STOVL within earshot of the big-deck U.S. Navy was keel hauled. The U.S. Air Force, with most of the world's research money, was convinced (wrongly, it turned out) that thrust reversers would allow its Advanced Tactical Fighter to use 1,500-foot runways. The Royal Air Force would be spending most of its money on Eurofighter for years to come.

As a result, it fell to pure research organizations to keep STOVL moving. In the United States, the main center of this work was NASA's Ames Research Center at Moffett Field on the edge of San Francisco Bay. The immense

40-by-80-foot, low-speed wind tunnel at Ames was ideal for research into STOVL and other projects that NASA grouped under the heading of "powered lift," and Ames was also a leader in the new art of computational fluid dynamics (CFD)—the use of supercomputers to model and predict aerodynamic performance.

In the United Kingdom, the Royal Aeronautical Establishment (later known as the Defence Research Agency, or DRA, and now part of the Defence Engineering Research Agency, or DERA) retained a strong interest in STOVL at its research sites at Farnborough and Bedford.

As members of a heretic minority, the British and American STOVL communities forged strong professional bonds, staging a biennial Powered Lift Conference that alternated between U.K. and U.S. locations. Since the high sheriffs in London and Washington regarded STOVL as unimportant, information flowed quite freely.

Between 1980 and 1985, NASA sponsored wind-tunnel work and theoretical studies on several STOVL concepts that had fallen out of the U.S. Navy's ill-fated supersonic V/STOL escapade. Broadly speaking, the U.S. Navy requirements from the 1970s were used as a yardstick to compare the different concepts.

In the United Kingdom, BAe's Warton design team built a full-scale mock-up of an ultra-STOL fighter with twin tilting engines, the P.103, and Kingston continued to work on PCB designs.

A great deal of basic research was performed on problems such as flight control and

The ultimate descendant of the original, United Kingdom–built small-wing Harrier was the Sea Harrier F/A.2. The pulse Doppler Blue Vixen radar is compatible with the AMRAAM missile, although this aircraft is carrying AIM-9s. Very apparent in this view are the Harrier's huge "elephant ear" inlets, which, pilots suspected, turned into airbrakes at high subsonic speeds. British Aerospace

The United Kingdom's Ministry of Defense funded the first large-scale test of plenum-chamber burning (PCB) above the ground and on an airplane. A PCB Pegasus prototype was reconditioned and installed in the recovered airframe of a crash-damaged Harrier, and the entire apparatus was suspended from an overhead gantry on the Shoeburyness firing range on the mudflats of the Thames estuary. British Aerospace

The PCB nozzles were of the droop-and-trail type and converged in vertical mode to produce a "fountain" effect, generating a rising column of hot air that helped support the aircraft. The potential for ground erosion was significant, and the high-speed exhaust generated heat and vibration in the airframe in cruising flight. British Aerospace

the complex interaction between the hot exhaust gases, the ground, and the airplane. The advent of fly-by-wire flight controls, reliable inertial sensors, and digital engine controls could make it easier to control a jet-lift airplane, but the sheer thrust involved in a supersonic design could make it more difficult. Aircraft-to-ground interactions were another good-news-and-bad-news story: New jet engines offered much more thrust per pound of weight than the Harrier's Pegasus, but the inevitable corollary was a hotter, faster exhaust that could buckle decks, soften and rip concrete, damage unprotected ears, and turn any loose object into a missile.

As this work continued, United States and United Kingdom leaders quietly worked to set up a formal joint program. At a conference at Farnborough in June 1983, four promising STOVL systems were identified as candidates for joint exploration. All were single-engine types and could be ready for service entry by 2000 to 2010, when the current STOVL fleet would need replacement. In discussions with the U.S. Marine Corps, Royal Air Force, and Royal Navy, a basic set of operational requirements was defined, allowing a fair comparison between the different concepts. Finally, a detailed agreement was drafted to protect national and company data. A memorandum of

Ralph Hooper's designs included the original P.1127 and Harrier—and the remarkable P.1216, one of the last BAe vectored-thrust designs. The twin-boom layout was chosen to keep the structure away from the destructive effects of the jet exhausts. The P.1216 was a single-engine design with a "three-post" engine, with two PCB front nozzles and a single-core nozzle. British Aerospace

Full-scale mock-up of the P.1216, under construction at Kingston in 1982. Weapons were to have been carried under the booms, which also accommodated the main landing gears. PCB studies continued until the late 1980s, until it became clear that there was no practical solution to ground erosion and signature problems. British Aerospace

understanding covering the U.K.–U.S. Advanced STOVL (ASTOVL) project was signed on a very wet day at Ames in January 1986.

Of the four chosen configurations, the most familiar was a P.1154-type design with a vectored thrust engine and PCB. It was well understood, but the noise, heat, and erosion caused by the exhaust was a problem, and the location of the engine at the midpoint of the airframe militated against supersonic efficiency. The location of the jet nozzles against the fuselage sides gave the aircraft an inherent IR signature problem.

Another simple approach was the Remote Augmented Lift System (RALS), which had been under study since the 1970s. RALS used a conventional rear-mounted engine with a vectoring nozzle; to balance the airplane in jet-borne flight, part of the air from the engine was ducted to a vertically mounted afterburner in the forward fuselage. RALS allowed you to build a STOVL fighter that looked a lot like a CTOL fighter, but the very hot, fast exhaust from the lift nozzle was intimidating.

Some NASA-Ames researchers favored the ejector principle, despite its failure on the XFV-12. The de Havilland Canada company had designed a different version of the concept, with large ejectors built into the roots of a delta wing,

The plan was to select the most promising of the four proposals for further investigation late in 1988. The United States and United Kingdom would then concentrate their resources on large-scale demonstrations of the chosen concept, with a view to being ready to start development of an operational aircraft in 1995.

Industry teams drew up preliminary designs around each system, explored their technical challenges, and measured them against the users' needs.

The Marines wielded the greatest influence on the requirement, and by 1987 they had made a significant decision: The advanced STOVL fighter would replace both the AV-8B and the F/A-18 so that the Marines would become an all-STOVL force, independent of the supercarriers. This meant that the Marines would be in the market for at least 600 STOVL

Alongside the studies of Harrier-type vectored thrust, the U.S.–U.K. industry teams formed as a result of a 1986 agreement looked at other concepts. This Lockheed Skunk Works design was based on the tandem-fan engine, with a two-section fan on a common shaft. In cruising flight, the engine acted as a conventional turbofan with a single inlet, mixed gas stream and exhaust. For takeoff and landing, though, the fan and the core were aerodynamically separate. Valves diverted the front fan exhaust through vectoring nozzles (Rolls-Royce designed a neat retractable vectoring nozzle), and auxiliary inlets opened to feed the core. The engine's bypass ratio and thrust were both increased, and the flow from the front nozzles was cool and slow. Lockheed

NASA returned to the ejector concept with support from General Dynamics and de Havilland Canada, which designed an F-16-like aircraft called the E-7. De Havilland built a large powered model of the E-7, and it was tested in 1987. The low-exhaust velocity was attractive, but the system was physically large, and the movement of a large air mass through the wing root during transition gave rise to interesting control issues. Bill Sweetman

and General Dynamics designed a STOVL fighter, the E-7, which used some F-16 components.

The fourth concept, drawing attention from Rolls-Royce and Lockheed, was the tandem-fan engine. This engine had two sets of fan stages, rotating on the same shaft, but separated by a long duct that incorporated valves and auxiliary inlets.

fighters, but it implied a tougher set of requirements, including air-to-air and all-weather attack capability. The U.S. Marine Corps decided to rebuild its AV-8Bs into an AV-8B Plus configuration, including a radar, so as to extend the Harrier II's life into the early 2000s, when an ASTOVL aircraft would be ready.

Key features of the requirement included a maximum operating weight empty of 24,000 pounds—the same as an F/A-18—supersonic speed, stealth characteristics (including the ability to carry some weapons internally), and an operating radius of 450 nautical miles (830 kilometers) with about 6,000 pounds (2,700 kilograms) of offensive weapons.

Even in 1987, therefore, recognizable parts of today's Joint Strike Fighter program were in place: the Anglo-American partnership, the Royal Navy, and U.S. Marine Corps commitment to the project and the cardinal points of the requirement. But there were real reasons why the project would not and could not leave the ground.

One was the secrecy surrounding stealth technology. Only a few of the people involved in the ASTOVL program were cleared to know about stealth, and they could not share this knowledge with others. Some of the competing concepts were less compatible with stealth than others, but those who knew this could not say so.

The principal problem, though, was that each of the concepts turned out to have a "showstopper"—an ineradicable limitation that was intolerable to the customer. The PCB engine was unworkable in terms of ground erosion and hot gas recirculation, and it was incompatible with stealth. RALS was a good way to dig a post hole. Nobody knew how to get the ejector concept to transition successfully, or how to build the complex valves in the heart of the tandem fan engine. And, apart from the Marines and the Royal Navy, nobody appeared to care.

By 1989, the ASTOVL effort seemed to be grinding to a halt, lost in a developmental valley of death. This made its revival, in the succeeding two years, appear almost miraculous.

Another important element of STOVL research in the 1980s was aimed at devising better control and piloting techniques. NASA-Ames operated this AV-8A for research into fully integrated flight and propulsion control, avoiding the need to jockey the throttle and vector control to stabilize the aircraft. It is seen in late 1987, hovering in front of the huge Navy airship sheds at Moffett Field. Bill Sweetman

27

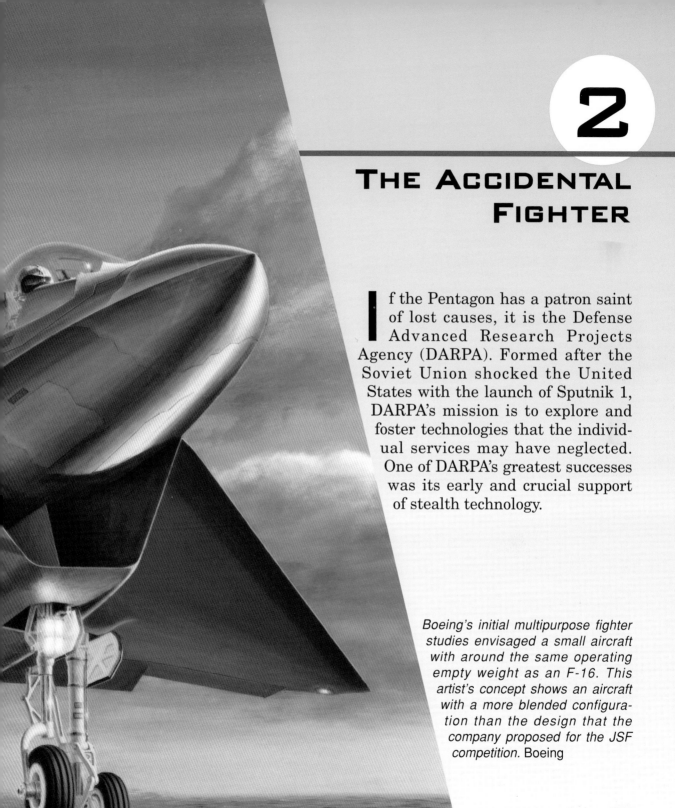

2

THE ACCIDENTAL
FIGHTER

If the Pentagon has a patron saint of lost causes, it is the Defense Advanced Research Projects Agency (DARPA). Formed after the Soviet Union shocked the United States with the launch of Sputnik 1, DARPA's mission is to explore and foster technologies that the individual services may have neglected. One of DARPA's greatest successes was its early and crucial support of stealth technology.

Boeing's initial multipurpose fighter studies envisaged a small aircraft with around the same operating empty weight as an F-16. This artist's concept shows an aircraft with a more blended configuration than the design that the company proposed for the JSF competition. Boeing

In the 1960s, too, the agency invented a way to use computers to share information about research and development efforts. It was called Arpanet and was the direct precursor of the Internet.

DARPA was involved in the U.S.–U.K. ASTOVL program since 1986. The director of DARPA's Advanced Systems Technology Office, Ron Murphy, had a long background in V/STOL (so much so that when he joined DARPA to run a classified program in 1984, many people assumed incorrectly that it was a V/STOL effort). In 1988, according to DARPA program manager Chuck Heber, the agency realized that the U.S.–U.K. program was in trouble and started working to generate some kind of requirement "since there was no way otherwise to go ahead." DARPA persuaded the Navy and the Marines to authorize a "desired operational capability document," an extremely tentative requirement. ("That and 50 cents buys you a cup of coffee," Heber would remark later.)

As DARPA worked to get an ASTOVL program started, Russia unveiled the Yakovlev Yak-141 naval STOVL fighter. Like the Yak-38, it had two forward-mounted lift-jets and a single lift/cruise engine. At the 1992 Farnborough air show, the Yak-141 made its first and only public appearance in the West. Observers noticed that, although the Yak-141 hovered, it did not land vertically, and speculated that any attempt to do so would have blown a hole in the Farnborough runway. Bill Sweetman

DARPA's emphasis was different from the U.S.–U.K. study in several important ways. The earlier study had set performance targets. DARPA's requirement made only two firm demands, both related to cost and operability: The aircraft should have an empty weight no higher than 24,000 pounds (10,900 kilograms)—a rough-and-ready way of capping the cost—and should take up no more room on a carrier deck than an F/A-18. Otherwise,

DARPA looked for the best possible balance of range, speed, and stealth.

Another difference was that DARPA wanted to build and fly a prototype as soon as possible. This was the key to achieving a breakthrough in stealth. The demonstrator served two roles: It persuaded the industry that there might be money in ASTOVL, and it forced the designers to offer solutions that were practical.

Another key feature of the DARPA requirement was that it was based on the General Electric F120 and Pratt and Whitney YF119 engines, then being tested on the Lockheed YF-22 and Northrop YF-23 Advanced Tactical Fighter (ATF) prototypes. These powerful engines opened up new approaches for ASTOVL designs—in particu-lar, they made it possible for an F-18-sized fighter with a single engine to land vertically without using afterburners.

From 1990 onward, the Pentagon increased DARPA's budgets and encouraged the agency to focus on making weapons more affordable. To help manage and promote the emerging ASTOVL project, DARPA hired a consultant, Dr. Bill Scheuren. A retired marine colonel who had been one of the first five Marine Corps officers to evaluate the Harrier, Scheuren would become a key player as DARPA sought support for a demonstrator program.

Between 1989 and 1991, DARPA funded aircraft design studies by McDonnell Douglas, General Dynamics, and Lockheed Advanced Development Company (the Skunk Works),

The Yak-141's powerful Soyuz R-79 lift/cruise engine was fitted with a three-bearing swiveling nozzle. The nozzle design retained a circular section throughout its length and was light and efficient. Lockheed Martin acquired Yakovlev data to help in the development of a similar nozzle for the JSF. The Yak-141 was tested in 1991 to 1993, but was grounded by 1994. Bill Sweetman

The large-scale powered model of Lockheed's Common Affordable Lightweight Fighter/ASTOVL design was completed in 1995. The design resembled a scaled-down version of the F-22, also designed at the Skunk Works: The principal differences were that the CALF had a single engine and a canard configuration. Canard solutions appeared attractive because they put the mass of the wing well aft. This was helpful in the vertical landing case, because it reduced the need to shift the center of thrust forward. From the aerodynamic viewpoint, it was desirable to move the wing aft, away from the bulge in the forebody caused by the lift fan bay. Lockheed Martin

together with propulsion studies at General Electric and Pratt and Whitney.

The studies concentrated on two basic problems with the earlier STOVL concepts. The first was that the hot, high-velocity exhaust gas was no longer a nuisance but a menace. The jet blast threatened to blow hapless swabs off the deck like confetti while creating a cloud of superheated air that would suck power out of the engine. Even if the challenge of hot-gas ingestion could be solved, operations on ship would be slowed down by the need to clear a large safety zone around a

landing aircraft. The second problem was that stealth appeared to mandate a single, rear-mounted exhaust nozzle in up-and-away flight.

Both these problems could be solved if there was a way to move some of the engine's total energy forward, to balance the rear-mounted nozzle, while increasing the system's mass flow and reducing its jet velocity.

Lockheed Skunk Works engineer Paul Bevilaqua devised such a method, which was patented in 1993. The new system evolved from the tandem fan, but with three principal differences: The forward fan stream was separate from the core airflow at all times; the fan was shut down in cruising flight; and the fan was rotated so that its axis was vertical. It was a less complex system than the tandem fan and had a more easily controlled transition.

At the same time, General Electric dusted off the data on lift fan systems that it had built for the U.S. Army in the 1960s. The General Electric fans were driven by turbines fed by engine exhaust gas. Consequently, these early DARPA studies emphasized fan-boosted systems.

In a parallel study, early in 1990, the U.S. Air Force's Flight Dynamics Laboratory issued STOVL study contracts to General Dynamics, McDonnell Douglas, Lockheed, and Northrop under the Advanced Fighter Technology Integration (AFTI) program, but canceled them a few months later when it became clear that Air Combat Command had no interest in STOVL for the planned F-16 replacement, the Multi-Role Fighter (MRF), but was concerned with greater range and stealth. In the process, however, some of the contractors had reopened the files on lift-plus-lift/cruise designs, with a separate jet engine to balance the aircraft and boost thrust in hovering flight.

The entire project was a pipe-dream until it could be funded. In order to allocate money for ASTOVL, DARPA needed a customer who would buy an ASTOVL aircraft if DARPA succeeded in inventing one that worked. The prime candidate was the U.S.

One of the most important F-22 features carried over to the Lockheed CALF design was its use of stealth technology. Lockheed had refined the faceted shape of the F-117, rounding most of the edges and adding curvature, resulting in a shape that was stealthy, aerodynamically efficient, and reasonably easy to manufacture. It also required minimal use of radar-absorbent material (RAM), most of which was concentrated in the wing and tail edges and the "chine" at the junction of the upper and lower surfaces. Bill Sweetman

The CALF model featured F-22-type inlets and adjustable leading-edge flaps to study stability and control issues in transition. The nonflying mock-up included a working propulsion system based on a Pratt and Whitney F100 engine. It also had a two-dimensional thrust-vectoring nozzle on the main engine; the lighter three-bearing nozzle came later. Lockheed Martin

Navy, which controlled the development of Marine Corps aircraft.

In the January 1991, the Navy's A-12 Avenger II bomber was canceled. With nothing else in sight to replace the aging A-6 and F-14, the Navy selected the F/A-18E/F Super Hornet to fill its carrier decks from 2000 onward and launched the new A-X program to provide a substitute long-range attack aircraft. Both the Super Hornet and A-X would be too large and too expensive for the U.S. Marine Corps.

Naval Air Systems Command (Navair) still regarded STOVL with distrust but could not legitimately ignore the need to replace aging Marine aircraft. At DARPA, program manager Heber, with Scheuren's support, lobbied the Navy to establish a Mission Element Needs Statement (MENS) for a STOVL fighter—the first step to an operational requirement. By late 1991 the Navy was drafting its MENS, and money for STOVL had been incorporated in DARPA's 1992 budget.

Later one of the DARPA managers expressed the view that the only reason Navair went along with the plan was that Navair expected the first round of studies to show that the STOVL fighter would not work. "We rolled them," he remarked. "Navair didn't expect a positive result."

DARPA laid out a plan for STOVL development. After about a year of competitive design studies, DARPA would choose two teams to carry out a three-year "critical technologies validation" (CTV) program running from March 1993 to March 1996, building and testing near-full-size, powered models of two ASTOVL designs. (This would avert the construction of a dud like the XFV-12A.)

In mid-1996, DARPA picked the most promising concept and awarded a contract to build and fly two prototypes by the end of 1999. At this point, the customer would be able to launch development of an operational aircraft at an acceptable level of risk.

Before the contracts were awarded, a new and very important element was added to the ASTOVL program. The DARPA team recognized that the fan-boosted ASTOVL concepts could be modified into a conventional fighter by removing the lift hardware and substituting a fuel tank. The result would be a fighter with a better range than the F-16, which was precisely what the U.S. Air Force wanted in an MRF.

The prospect of replacing the Marines' F/A-18s and AV-8s and the U.S. Air Force F-16s with a common aircraft was important because it linked ASTOVL to DARPA's strategic goal of making weapons less costly. A dual-service fighter could save tens of billions of

As part of its ASTOVL research in the 1980s, NASA commissioned the Outdoor Aerodynamic Research Facility (OARF) at the Ames Research Center near Palo Alto, California. The OARF permitted ASTOVL propulsion and control systems to be tested in the hover mode at full power, with some freedom in pitch and roll. Lockheed Martin

In this OARF test of the CALF model, dye streaks on the tarmac show how the fan exhaust generates a high-velocity airflow along the ground, radiating from the center of the exhaust stream. The line of shortened streaks, to the right of the main star-shaped pattern, shows how the fan exhaust prevents the hot airflow from the main exhaust from making its way forward to the inlet. Lockheed Martin

dollars in research, development, and production. The project acquired a new name: Common Affordable Lightweight Fighter (CALF).

The first CALF contracts were awarded to McDonnell Douglas and Lockheed in March 1993. Both companies proposed stealthy canard designs, with internal bays for two 2,000-pound (900-kilogram) bombs and a pair of AIM-120 air-to-air missiles, and with auxiliary lift fans located behind the cockpit.

Lockheed's design used a modified Pratt and Whitney F119 engine. A clutch immediately in front of the engine connected the low-pressure shaft to a driveshaft, which drove an Allison-developed fan. McDonnell Douglas planned to use a version of the GE F120, modified to allow

high-pressure air to be bled from the compressor. The air would be ducted forward to the lift-fan's turbine. In both concepts, the total airflow was almost doubled in the vertical-lift mode, boosting low-speed thrust while reducing jet velocity.

Both teams designed prototype aircraft that could be built in two versions—one with its lift system and one without. The designation X-32 was assigned: The CTOL aircraft would be the X-32A, and the STOVL aircraft would be the X-32B, whichever team was selected.

From the outset, DARPA planned to involve the United Kingdom in the program. After some delays due to the sensitivity of stealth technology, the United Kingdom formally joined the effort in early 1994. British Aerospace, long associated with McDonnell Douglas on the Harrier program, teamed with the U.S. company to support ASTOVL.

Defense contractors can smell blood in the water from miles away. CALF was an outside bet because there was still no formal requirement for an ASTOVL aircraft or a CTOL derivative in early 1993, but the potential jackpot was large enough to bring two more contenders into the fray.

Boeing had started looking at future fighters as soon as the Advanced Tactical Fighter award went to Lockheed in April 1991. Having placed fourth in the ATF demonstration/validation contest in 1986, Boeing was determined to establish itself as a prime contractor

for fighters. Certain that future budgets would be tight, Boeing focused on low cost. The company concluded that what was needed was a multiservice, multipurpose fighter with an empty weight close to that of an F-16, a price far lower than the F-22, STOVL capability to replace the Harrier, and a better range than in-service fighters.

Boeing's concentration on cost and simplicity defined the design that emerged from a study of 30 configurations. It was a direct-lift design with no separate lift fan. To minimize weight and accommodate a large fuel load, Boeing selected a delta wing. Although it did not win either of the DARPA contracts, the company had enough faith in its concept to take part in the ground-test program with its

The Lockheed Martin CALF model under test in NASA's 80-by-120-foot low-speed wind-tunnel at Ames Research Center. The tunnel's test section was expanded in the early 1980s to support tests of full-size STOVL and STOL aircraft. Lockheed Martin

By 1996, when tests started in the NASA tunnel, Lockheed Martin had modified the CALF model to represent the JAST design by removing the canard foreplanes and adding a close-coupled aft stabilizer—again, a layout borrowed from the F-22. The vented-D nozzle of the lift fan, which extends from the lift-fan bay to deflect its thrust rearward for STOL acceleration and transition, is visible here. Lockheed Martin

funds. Like McDonnell Douglas and Lockheed, the company built a large-scale powered model and tested it on a large outdoor rig.

Northrop Grumman announced its intention to bid on CALF in the summer of 1994. The company selected a lift-plus-lift/cruise design. It had an F119 fitted with a vectoring nozzle and a separate lift-fan engine in the forward fuselage. Rolls-Royce joined the team to work on the lift engine. The design featured an unusual hammerhead wing planform, with a small canard attached to a large fixed leading-edge extension. Northrop did not intend to build a powered model, arguing that the risks of the lift-plus-lift/cruise configuration were small. In fact, a lift-plus-lift/cruise supersonic STOVL fighter had already flown: Russia's Yakovlev Yak-141, the existence of which was disclosed in 1991.

Meanwhile, seismic shifts in Pentagon policy were about to change the CALF program beyond all recognition.

The 1992 presidential election ended 12 years of Republican rule and brought new leadership to the Pentagon. One figure stood head and shoulders above a mostly mediocre group of appointees: Dr. Bill Perry, who returned to the Pentagon as deputy secretary of defense and became defense secretary in early 1994 after Les Aspin resigned. Known as "the godfather of stealth" because of his role in launching the original stealth programs in the late 1970s, Perry was an entrepreneur and engineer who realized that Cold War business-as-usual was dead.

From now on, Perry believed, the United States would not buy one system for each service. Moreover, the Pentagon could not sustain half-a-dozen prime contractors in each line of business. The push toward joint-service programs went in parallel with industrial consolidation, and tactical aircraft would not be exempt.

In September 1993, the Pentagon leadership issued a "bottom-up review" of defense programs. The Air Force's MRF and the A/F-X—a joint-service deep-strike fighter—were canceled. Instead, the Pentagon established a new program: Joint Advanced Strike Technology (JAST). The JAST office was to define and develop aircraft, weapon, and sensor technologies that would support the development of future tactical aircraft.

McDonnell Douglas proposed this lean and rakish CALF/ASTOVL design with strong wing-body blending, small vertical tails, and diamond-shaped wing and canard. The lift/cruise engine, based on General Electric's F120, featured a pitch/yaw vectoring nozzle for up-and-away flight, and side nozzles for STOVL operations. High-pressure air was bled from the compressor to drive the lift fan. McDonnell Douglas

JAST was a new concept, and in the first few months of its existence, nobody was quite sure what it was. In December 1993, when the Anglo-American ASTOVL community held its biennial conference in Santa Clara, California, speakers avoided linking JAST with DARPA's CALF program. CALF was clearly a prime example of what JAST was supposed to do, but the ASTOVL advocates—with a flight demonstration program almost within their grasp—feared that Congress or the Pentagon would de-fund CALF and assign its goals to the JAST office, where ASTOVL might languish on a back burner for years.

Alternatively, JAST and CALF could be seen as complementary; while JAST would focus on operational issues, weapons, and sensors, CALF was strictly an aircraft and propulsion demonstration. Other people in the industry were openly critical of JAST, worried that it would turn into an "engineering sandbox," which would fritter resources on new ideas that would not reflect the users' operational needs.

Those who doubted that JAST would amount to anything reckoned without the program's first director, Air Force Major General George Muellner. A 5,300-hour fighter pilot

After McDonnell Douglas joined forces with British Aerospace and Northrop Grumman, the team abandoned the gas-driven lift fan and the canard layout. By October 1995, the team was tunnel-testing this design, with a W-shaped wing trailing edge, four tail surfaces, and a separate lift engine behind the cockpit. McDonnell Douglas

The JAST office adopted state-of-the-art industrial processes and tools to pursue its ambitious goals. The many elements of the program were organized into integrated product teams (IPTs), which combined engineers, production, and maintenance experts from the contractors and the customers: The goal was to avoid designing technically inspiring devices that were too expensive to produce or impossible to maintain. JAST would be designed on computers, using commercially available design tools, and the JAST team enthusiastically adopted the Internet and the Web as tools of communication.

Another important tool was distributed, interactive simulation. The JAST office conducted war games that involved experts and resources from all services and throughout the United States, connected by satellite. This made it possible to evaluate the actual benefits of the airplane's performance to the joint-

with 690 combat missions over Vietnam in F-4s, Muellner had once commanded the 6513th Test Squadron based at the Air Force's secret flight-test center in Groom Lake, Nevada. In the Gulf War, Muellner assembled and led the scratch unit of Air Force and civilian technicians, which took the experimental Joint STARS radar surveillance system into action.

By the fall of 1994, CALF was indeed about to be absorbed by JAST, but under Muellner's leadership it had become JAST's centerpiece. Muellner's vision was to create a family of aircraft to embrace all the operational needs that were to have been met by CALF, A/F-X, and MRF. Using new technology to reduce costs in development, manufacture, and operation, the JAST family would have the performance and survivability to perform deep-strike missions but would be affordable enough to replace F-16s both in the United States and overseas. The result would be a "universal fighter" that could be built in thousands, further reducing costs.

As McDonnell Douglas redesigned its JAST design in 1995–96, a strong influence was the X-36 unmanned experimental aircraft. The company's Phantom Works had won NASA and DARPA support for what was then a secret program in 1993, and it was unveiled in 1996. Clearly related to the original CALF design, it featured a yaw-only vectoring nozzle with no external moving parts and split brake/rudder/elevon surfaces, and it had no vertical tail surfaces. McDonnell Douglas

Combining the X-36 no-tail technology with the lift-plus-lift/cruise design, McDonnell Douglas' final JSF submission was sleeker and more stealthy-looking than either of its rivals. The unusual "lambda" wing shape was reminiscent of the B-2, while the control philosophy and stealth design strongly recalled the Northrop/McDonnell Douglas YF-23. The pitch/yaw vectoring nozzle was used in up-and-away flight, and retractable vectoring nozzles beneath the fuselage were used for takeoff and landing. McDonnell Douglas

force campaign. Was it worth increasing the range at the expense of maximum Mach number? What was the actual value of a longer-range radar? The war-gaming tools provided a consistent answer.

Tools such as this were critical as the customer services—the Marines, the U.S. Air Force, the U.S. Navy, and soon, the Royal Navy—began to hammer out a joint requirement. If there was one element of JAST that aroused skepticism and hostility, it was the idea that one aircraft could work for every service. The last time this was tried at the Pentagon's direction, the result was the F-111. The Navy rejected the aircraft, leaving the Air Force with

an aircraft burdened with design compromises.

In the case of JAST, it seemed impossible that the Navy's deep-strike fighter and the Air Force's F-16 replacement could be remotely similar. But any aircraft powered by a modified F119 or F120 was not exactly small, and the long range required by the Air Force was close to the Navy's needs.

One of Muellner's priority tasks was to investigate the Navy's unshakable insistence on a twin-engined aircraft. The JAST office sponsored an exhaustive analysis of the one-versus-two-engine issue, performed by Georgia Tech Research Institute and Johns Hopkins University—academic engineering centers

McDonnell Douglas proposed to fit the U.S. Air Force and Navy versions of its JSF design with larger tails, outer wings, and high-lift devices to handle higher weights. The W-shaped trailing edge recalled the company's F-101 Voodoo fighter of the 1950s. McDonnell Douglas

with, respectively, long-standing Air Force and Navy links. The conclusion was that the single-engined aircraft would be equal or better in terms of survivability. The only time that a twin can survive a hit that would down a single-engine type is if one engine is knocked out, but the other engine and all other vital systems are left intact. The studies showed that this would hardly ever happen. (It did not work that way for Muellner, who ejected from a battle-damaged F-4 over Vietnam.)

It took more than studies and simulation, though, to persuade the services to buy commonality. Hard reality did the job. The Navy needed a stealth aircraft. The Marines' AV-8Bs were not getting younger. The Air Force would not maintain even its post-1993 force size without a low-cost F-16 replacement. Individual leaders might have their reservations about Muellner's vision, but they had no alternatives either.

By the spring of 1995, the JAST train was moving at express speed. In an interview in

April, Muellner said that the customers had converged on a family of closely similar designs, different mainly in the way that they landed and took off.

CALF was very important in this process, acting as the nucleus around which the JAST requirement formed. The work already done by DARPA and its contractors pointed to a common solution for the Marines and the U.S. Air Force. The single-versus-twin study removed the main obstacle in the way of adapting the design to meet the Navy's needs.

In the process, though, the demonstration program changed. JAST was oriented toward the requirements of three U.S. customers. CALF/ASTOVL had been driven by the Marine Corps, and the Air Force and Navy had never defined a formal requirement for it. Performance and other specifications would change to meet the other services' needs.

CALF/ASTOVL had operational goals, but its formal objective was to demonstrate technology for a STOVL system. JAST was aimed at reducing risks for a military aircraft and included many elements beyond the ASTOVL systems. The flight demonstrators would not carry these technologies, but would represent a design that would accommodate them.

JAST was directly linked to an engineering, manufacturing, and development (EMD) program. In order to keep the project competitive, the JAST office decided to fly prototypes of two designs. (DARPA had planned to fly only one.) The "down-select" to two candidates was set for the summer of 1996.

The industrial implications were enormous. The Marines wanted to replace 600 older aircraft, the Navy needed 300 aircraft, and the Air Force could replace almost 2,000 F-16s. Never had such a massive program been created so fast. Moreover, JAST looked like the only U.S. tactical aircraft program that would start before 2010. In 1986, seven companies had submitted proposals for the ATF Dem/Val phase. By late 1994, four companies were

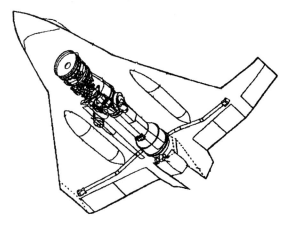

An early impression of Boeing's CALF design shows the original wingtip-mounted fins and rudders. These were designed to act as winglets, giving the aerodynamic benefits of greater wingspan while keeping the aircraft compact. The company later determined that conventional twin tails were lighter. Boeing

ready to compete in JAST. Grumman had been acquired by Northrop, General Dynamics had been absorbed by Lockheed (which was itself in the process of merging with Martin-Marietta), and Rockwell had virtually left the military aircraft business. The two companies to be eliminated in 1996 were out of the picture as combat aircraft primes.

Late in 1994, Northrop Grumman agreed to collaborate with McDonnell Douglas and BAe on JAST. The three companies formed a "dream team" that encompassed all the Western world's STOVL experience, both the surviving groups with carrier-based fighter skills: Northrop's stealth technology and Grumman's expertise in all-weather strike systems.

Boeing and Lockheed talked about teaming, which would have left only two teams to bid for the two prototype contracts, but the JAST program office said that it did not want to review multiple designs from each team: Each team would have to agree on a single design. Neither Boeing nor Lockheed would give up its own design, so the companies did not team up.

Many people—including some McDonnell Douglas people at St. Louis—considered the result to be a foregone conclusion. Boeing had never built a manned supersonic airplane or a jet fighter, had not delivered a production fighter of any kind since President Roosevelt's first term and (as far as anyone still knows), and had never built a stealth aircraft. The other teams had vastly greater experience.

By mid-1995, however, all was clearly not well with the McDonnell Douglas team. McDonnell Douglas announced in June (only a year before the planned down-select date) that its JAST design would use Northrop Grumman's lift-plus-lift/cruise (LPLC) concept. The nearly completed large-scale powered model of the gas-driven lift-fan design was mothballed. One reason for the change was that the gas-driven system required large hot-gas ducts through the mid-fuselage. The LPLC layout allowed that critical section of the aircraft to be more similar in the STOVL and CTOL versions, and studies also had shown consistently that LPLC was the lightest solution.

But LPLC had some substantial drawbacks. The Marine Corps's logistics community hated the idea of a fighter with two different engines. "The logistics people start climbing the walls, and rightly," Scheuren said in 1991. "The care and feeding of one engine is bad enough." Another disadvantage was reliability. On one mission, an LPLC fighter has three engine cycles—the lift/cruise engine starts and stops once, and the lift engine twice—but unlike a conventional twin-engined fighter, it cannot land on the ship if either engine fails.

McDonnell Douglas could argue that its design would enter service with a thoroughly proven lift/cruise engine (a standard F119) and that the lift engine was little more complex than Lockheed Martin's lift fan, but it was an uphill struggle. Moreover, the demonstrator aircraft would require a brand-new lift engine.

Lockheed Martin also unveiled a revised JAST design in late 1995. The major difference stemmed from the Navy's carrier-landing requirements. A carrier-based aircraft must be able to fly slowly in a flat attitude, which implies a generous wingspan and effective flaps, and must feature responsive and precise control at low speeds. As Lockheed Martin adapted the canard design to these requirements, the canard became awkwardly big.

Anticanard prejudice played a role. Lockheed had relocated the JAST program to Fort Worth, where F-16 designer Harry Hillaker had long taught that "the optimum location for a canard is on somebody else's airplane." In 1995, the canard Eurofighter Typhoon was sitting on the ground while its designers wrestled with flight-control problems, and the Saab Gripen's developers were dealing with a rash of handling gremlins. All in all, the Lockheed Martin team felt that there was enough risk in the JAST program without adding a canard to the mix.

Lockheed Martin looked at a pure delta wing—at one point, the company was looking at a delta for the U.S. Marine Corps, U.S. Air Force, and Royal Navy and a tailed configuration for the U.S. Navy—but the final design echoed the F-22, with four tails and a cropped delta wing. Data from the large-scale powered model, unveiled in April 1995 and tested at NASA Ames, was still applicable.

Boeing took the challenge of the Navy requirement head-on, without changing its basic design. Instead, the company scaled the airplane up, fitted extended wingtips in place of tip-mounted fins, and employed a range of high-lift devices to reduce approach speeds.

The McDonnell Douglas team did not show its definitive design in early 1996. Its most radical feature was that it was a "near-tailless" airplane, with only a vestige of vertical tail area provided by a shallow V-tail. Basic control and stability would be provided by split air brake-rudder surfaces on the wing trailing edges, and combat agility would be provided by a lightweight, all-axis, thrust-vectoring nozzle, developed by Pratt and Whitney.

In March 1996, the JAST office released a request for proposals for the JAST prototypes, with a deadline in early June. Shortly afterward, the project's name changed from JAST to the Joint Strike Fighter (JSF), reflecting the fact that it was backed by an operational requirement.

The JSF announcement was first set for late October, then slipped to November 16, after the presidential election. Briefing the media at the 1996 Farnborough air show, the McDonnell Douglas team seemed sure of success. Other observers (including the author) were less sure of the outcome.

In earlier two-track demonstrator programs, such as the Lightweight Fighter and Advanced Medium STOL Transport projects in the 1970s and the Advanced Tactical Fighter in the 1980s, the evaluators had consistently picked candidates that were different from one another and had shown a tendency to select one low-risk candidate and one that offered greater payoffs but relied on innovative technology. For example, the Northrop YF-17 was a twin-engined aircraft with conventional flight controls, while the GD YF-16 was a single-engine, fly-by-wire design. In that evaluation, Boeing's LWF placed second to the F-16, but it was not chosen because it was too like the F-16; and the YF-17 would demonstrate a different approach to the requirement.

If the JSF evaluators followed this pattern, it was Boeing that was a sure bet. Boeing was offering a simpler airplane without the auxiliary lift system of the other two designs and with a very different wing, engine location, and inlet. Overall, too, the Boeing JSF was regarded as a high-risk design—if any of a number of features did not work properly, the airplane might fail to meet key areas of the requirement.

This left Lockheed Martin and McDonnell Douglas in contention for the other contract and, if the evaluators stayed with the pattern, they would select the less risky design to back up the radical Boeing approach. McDonnell Douglas was relying on an untried control system and a paper lift engine; Lockheed Martin

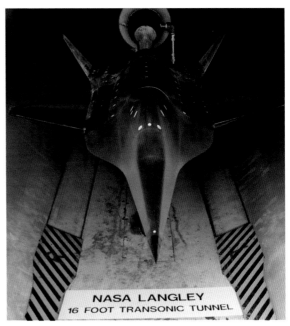

Among the Multi-Role Fighter (MRF) designs produced before the JAST program started was this concept, tested in NASA Langley's wind tunnel. This is believed to be a McDonnell Douglas design. NASA

had ground-tested its powered-lift system, and the aerodynamic and stealth features of its design were based solidly on F-22 data.

The evaluators indeed followed this logic. Defense Secretary Bill Perry announced that Boeing and Lockheed Martin would build JSF prototypes and compete to build the production aircraft.

The decision caused shock in St. Louis, where McDonnell Douglas corporate leaders had concluded only weeks earlier that the company's commercial aircraft business was in an irrevocable decline. The JSF loss meant that the company's share of the military market was also, in the long term, headed downward. Weeks after the JSF announcement, McDonnell Douglas and Boeing disclosed that the two companies had agreed to merge. Not one piece of a flyable aircraft had been produced, but JSF had already made its mark on aerospace history.

3

THE GREAT COMPROMISE

O ne engineer who has worked around the JSF program for many years observed that its size and significance can be compared to the intercontinental ballistic missile (ICBM) project of the 1950s. It is not much of an exaggeration.

Simulation is an extremely important tool in JSF development. High-speed communications have made it possible to interlink simulators and other computers, and their users, across the United States in real time. The "pilot" in this simulation, wearing a helmet-mounted display and using large-format color cockpit displays, could be taking part in a campaign-level simulation involving large friendly and hostile forces. McDonnell Douglas

A full-scale mock-up of the U.S. Air Force version of Lockheed Martin's JSF design completed in 1998. The family resemblance to the F-22 is clear, with a sharp chine line along the fuselage. The weapons bay doors are visible forward of the main landing gear, which retracts forward into the wing-body junction. This means that the Navy fighter's heavier landing gear can be accommodated without changing the primary structure. Lockheed Martin

No fighter project in recent history has started with a verifiable 3,000-aircraft requirement. Indeed, if JSF continues as a winner-take-all program, the victor will dominate military aviation until most of the people reading this book have retired. The project is revolutionary, in a number of ways, and, like the ICBM, threatens established empires and ways of doing business.

The JSF family is intended to include a STOVL derivative without inflating the cost and degrading the performance of its conventional siblings, a notion that nobody would have taken seriously for a second before 1990. The JSF project takes aim at the idea that cost, in a military program, cannot be controlled as tightly as it is in the development of an airliner. It is the first project of its size to be conducted in a totally joint-service—"purple"—environment. This is true revolution, and in 1999 (as these words are written) nobody really knows how it can all be accomplished.

There are three main strands of activity within the JSF program. In the most visible part of the project, Lockheed Martin and Boeing are each designing and building two Concept Demonstration Aircraft (CDAs). The CDAs have three principal tasks: They will prove the design's up-and-away performance characteristics (stealth characteristics will be validated by model tests), demonstrate the low-speed performance required for carrier landings, and prove that the STOVL concept works.

The CDAs are designated in the X-series, in alphabetical order, so that Boeing's JSF is the X-32 (re-using the CALF designation) and

The Lockheed Martin STOVL variant in Royal Navy markings, launching a British Aerospace Advanced Short-Range AAM (ASRAAM). The upper body shape behind the cockpit has been made wider to accommodate the lift fan beneath two folding doors, and the rear of the canopy frame is different from the U.S. Air Force and Navy aircraft. Like the auxiliary engine inlet doors above the fuselage, the lift-fan doors are aligned with the wing edges in accordance with stealth design principles. Control surface edges are sculpted in "cat's-eye" fashion to avoid RCS glints as they move. Lockheed Martin

49

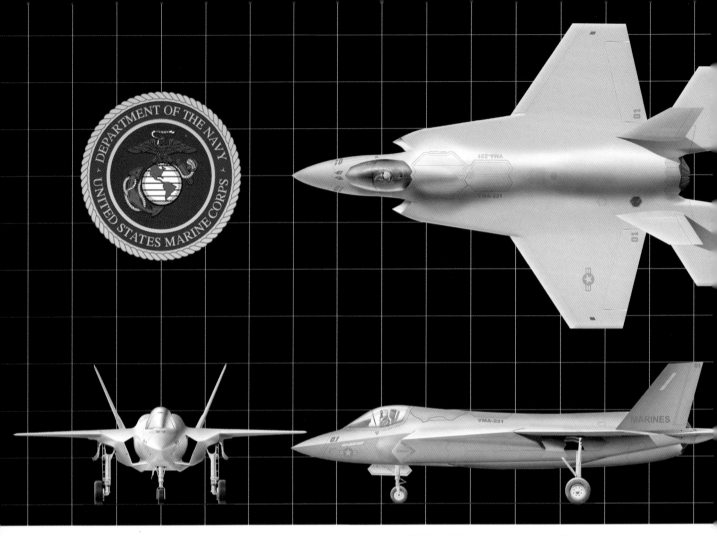

By late 1998, Lockheed Martin reached the third version of its PWSC JSF design, and the differences between the Air Force Design 230-3A and the Navy Design 230-3C became greater. Driven by a tough Navy requirement for bring-back weight and approach speed, the Navy variant's wing had grown almost as large as an F-15's wing, and the horizontal tails had grown in proportion. Greater weight has also demanded a stronger and heavier landing gear. Meanwhile, the wing of the Air Force and STOVL versions has been made shorter and broader, so that the STOVL aircraft no longer needs wing folding. Lockheed Martin

the Lockheed Martin aircraft is the X-35. The JSF office avoided using "YF" designations to emphasize that there was no "fly-off," and no commitment to select the better-performing CDA. Ideally, the CDAs would demonstrate that either team's definitive JSF design would work; the Pentagon would then select a winner based on a balance of operational utility and cost. Both team's CDA prototypes will be powered by modified F119 engines—a selection made by default, because the F119 is the only flight-rated engine with enough power to do the job.

The second major part of JSF is the design of each competitor's Preferred Weapon System Concept (PWSC). The PWSC includes the design of an operational JSF, detailed proposals for production and support, and a plan for

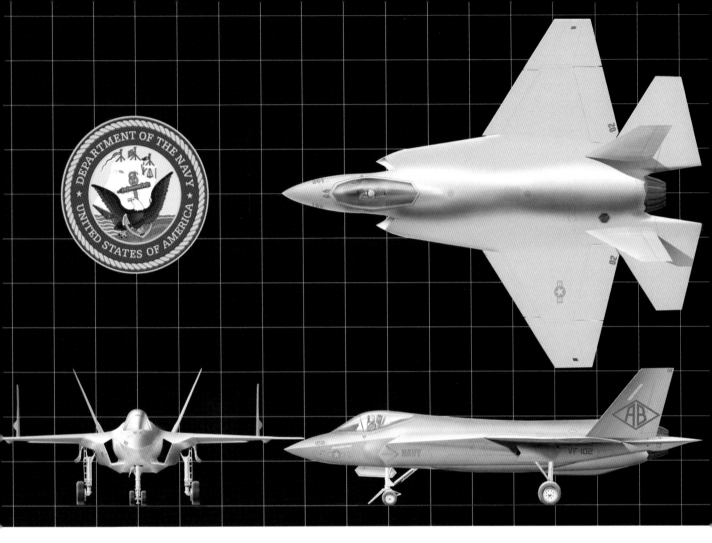

the engineering and manufacturing development (EMD) stage.

The third sector of JSF consists of a variety of technology programs. Some elements of this work predate JAST. For instance, the Joint Integrated Subsystems Technology (J/IST) demonstration has its roots in Air Force research into electrical actuation for flight controls. Others, including much of the avionics activity, were launched in the early days of JAST when it was realized that their effect on cost was decisive.

The JSF office itself will continue to refine and develop the requirements. The JSF is the first aircraft to be designed in the era of campaign-level simulation so that changes to the requirements can be tested in the Virtual Strike Warfare Environment (VSWE), a joint-service tool that evaluates how changes affect the outcomes of various military operations.

The JSF acquisition plan makes it clear that the performance targets on which the CDA designs were based were not final. It laid out a process by which the service customers would look at the progress of the CDA designs, the different technology programs, and the evolving threat, and produce a series of Joint Interim Requirements Documents (JIRDs).

In earlier programs, the customer set the requirement, the contractor tried to meet it,

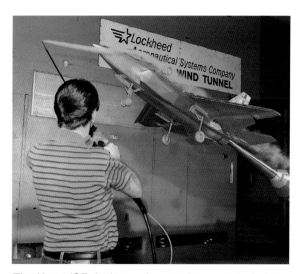

The Navy JSF design undergoes low-speed wind-tunnel testing. By enlarging the leading-edge and trailing-edge flaps, and by adding outer folding panels and ailerons, Lockheed Martin has been able to increase the size of the Navy airplane's wing without changing the wing-body junction. The X-35 prototypes will both be convertible to Navy use. Lockheed Martin

and the cost was a by-product of this process. JSF inverted this process. The cost could and would be controlled independently, and the contractor and customer would agree on what could be designed and built for the money. A cardinal rule was that the cost impact of any change to the requirements had to be fully evaluated. If any change resulted in a cost increase, an equal savings had to be found somewhere else, and this is the main reason for the annual issue of a revised JIRD.

JIRD I was produced in 1995 and focused on size, speed, and stealth—the factors that determine the airplane's shape. JIRD II, issued in June 1997, looked at major trades between performance, cost, and supportability. JIRD III, released in the fall of 1998, addressed a range of issues including supportable stealth technology, adverse weather, night capability, and mission planning. These will lead to the final Joint Operational Requirements Document

(JORD), which is due to be released in December 1999. Most of the technology programs will have made their final reports a year earlier.

The final showdown will start in 2000, as the CDA aircraft go through their flight tests, with the release of the request for proposals for the EMD program. The Pentagon is due to pick a winner at the end of 2000, and the 80-month EMD phase will start in March 2001. EMD and production will be partially concurrent; production will start in 2006, and the first operational aircraft will be delivered some time in 2008.

The only cast-iron guarantee applying to these dates is that they will change, particularly since the planned decision date will fall under a lame-duck administration.

Also subject to change are the numbers of aircraft required. Nominally, the U.S. Air Force needs about 2,000 aircraft to replace F-16s; however, some serious interest is reported in a small force of ASTOVL aircraft to replace A-10s. The U.S. Navy's stated requirement is for 300 aircraft, but 1997's Quadrennial Defense Review eliminated 442 Navy F/A-18E/Fs, leaving 400 aircraft slots that could be filled either by JSF or the Super Hornet.

The Marine Corps requires 600 STOVL aircraft to replace AV-8Bs and F/A-18s; this requirement has remained consistent. The Royal Navy and Royal Air Force will need at least 60 aircraft to meet its Future Carrier-Based Aircraft (FCBA) requirement, forming a joint force that will replace Royal Navy and RAF Harriers.

Three key concepts underpin JSF. The first is the assumption that other aircraft will take care of the most severe air-to-air threats. The U.S. Air Force and Navy do not require JSF to be their primary air-to-air fighter, do not need to pay for such a capability, and do not want JSF to be perceived as an alternative to the F-22 or Super Hornet.

Although the F stands for fighter, the initial requirement was 70 percent weighted

The standard reference weapon for the Air Force and Navy JSF versions is the 2,000-pound (900-kilogram) Boeing GBU-31 Joint Direct Attack Munition (JDAM). It has a simple GPS/inertial guidance system that is programmed, immediately before release, with the trajectory calculated by the fighter's weapon computers. The result is that the weapon compensates for bombing errors caused by wind and other factors. JDAM is not as accurate as a laser-guided bomb, but it is much less expensive and is autonomous after release. By the time JSF enters service, the Air Force plans to have developed an inexpensive seeker for JDAM, which will automatically guide the weapon on to a selected target. Lockheed Martin

toward air-to-ground missions. The Lockheed Martin X-35, for instance, has a higher wing loading than the F-22 and no in-flight vectored thrust. The JSF's standard AAM is not the AIM-9X Sidewinder, but the AIM-120 Advanced Medium Range Air-to-Air Missiles (AMRAAM)—better for self-defense than for dogfighting. (In Lockheed Martin's design, the AAM locations are not even suitable for an AIM-9X, because the airframe blocks much of the seeker's field of view.)

The second principle of the requirement is first-day stealth, which allows the aircraft to perform its first missions as a stealth aircraft, with a modest weapon load, and then carry more ordnance as the campaign continues and the defenses are beaten down. In this way, JSF can be stealthy and yet can deliver

The large canopy makes the JSF look smaller than it is: In fact, the fighter has more installed thrust than an F/A-18. The canopy looks large because it has an unusually low sill line. The CV version meets Navy requirements for over-the-nose visibility, while the STOVL version must have good downward-and-sideways visibility, for obstacle clearance in a vertical landing. Lockheed Martin

enough weapons to handle the expected number of targets. Both designs incorporate four large-capacity external hard points for extra fuel and weapons.

The other key concept is that the Pentagon expects to have retired its dumb bombs by the time JSF enters service. JSF's least accurate weapons will be standard Boeing GBU-31/32 Joint Direct Attack Munitions (JDAMs) with an accuracy of 33 feet (10 meters), and, by 2008, a low-cost precision seeker should also be available. The result is that a small weapon load on JSF will be as effective as a much larger load of unguided weapons.

The Boeing X-32 and Lockheed Martin X-35

are very different from each other, but are designed to meet the same basic set of requirements. All three services require an internal load of two JDAMs and two AMRAAMs. The Navy and Air Force want to carry the 2,000-pound (900-kilogram) GBU-31 and the Marine Corps is content with the 1,000-pound (450-kilogram) GBU-32. In 1998, the three services resolved the vexed question of a gun: The U.S. Air Force version will have an internal gun, while the Marines and Navy aircraft can be fitted with a gun pack that will fit into the weapon bay, displacing one of the JDAMs.

Range requirements vary: The Marine Corps and Air Force have a required unrefueled radius of 450 nautical miles (830 kilometers) and a desired range of 550 nautical miles (1,020 kilometers), but the Navy requires 550 nautical miles (1,020 kilometers) as a minimum. All three require speed and maneuverability "comparable" to current fighters, without rigidly specifying numbers.

As for stealth, the U.S. Navy is most demanding because Navy JSFs will be the service's only stealthy aircraft and will have to penetrate the toughest defenses with minimal support. The U.S. Air Force expects to have B-2s, F-117s, and strike-configured F-22s for this mission, so its standards are not as high. The

The Lockheed Martin JSF's diverterless inlet is clearly visible on this forebody wind-tunnel model. The inlet, patented in 1998, is an ingenious concept. It has no slots, diverters or apertures, which are a problem in terms of stealth. Instead, a bump on the body side creates a local pressure rise. When the slow, turbulent boundary layer of air that forms close to the body encounters the pressure rise, it splits like water flowing around a stone. The raked inlet lips capture the smooth outer airflow while permitting the boundary layer to flow away from the inlet. Also visible here is a fence, which controls the airflow into the lift fan. Lockheed Martin

Lockheed Martin JSF Propulsion Concept (STOVL)

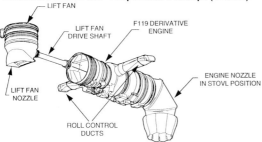

LIFT FAN

LIFT FAN
DRIVE SHAFT

F119 DERIVATIVE
ENGINE

ENGINE NOZZLE
IN STOVL POSITION

LIFT FAN
NOZZLE

ROLL CONTROL
DUCTS

The shaft-driven lift-fan propulsion system is designed to boost thrust and reduce jet velocity while providing a smooth transition between STO, up-and-away, and VL modes. The main components are the fan, its drive system, and the main engine. Both the fan and main engine have vectoring nozzles. In the powered-lift mode, the engine's primary nozzle is opened, reducing back pressure and allowing the low-pressure turbine to do more work: This excess power is transferred from the shaft to the lift fan. The shaft extracts 27,000 shaft horsepower (20 megawatts) from the engine, almost twice as much power as any other airborne shaft-turbine engine. Meanwhile, the exhaust from the engine's front fan passes into two large roll-control ducts, which extend into the wing roots. Pratt and Whitney

Marine Corps' primary mission is visual close air support with external weapons, so stealth is less important; however, primary features of the design that make stealth attainable (shape and internal stores) are inherent to the basic structure of the airplane and will be included on all versions.

The JSF is expected to be able to perform precision attacks at night, under the weather and, to some extent, against targets that are obscured by fog, rain, or clouds. Stealth rules out external pods, so the necessary electronic and optical sensors must be carried internally.

The JSF requirements represent a challenge. The most basic conflict concerns the Marine/Royal Navy STOVL requirement and the Navy's weapon load and mission radius. The STOVL version needs to land vertically at the end of its mission, with reserve fuel and unused

weapons. This limits its empty weight to a proportion of engine thrust, which in turn is limited by the power of a derivative F119 and drives the designer to the smallest, lightest possible aircraft. But the Navy aircraft needs to carry a heavy load of weapons and fuel and a big wing for carrier approaches, together with the extra structural strength required to withstand the shock of catapult launches and arrested landings. Advanced, exotic technology might do the job but is ruled out by the target price: $28 million in 1995 dollars for the Air Force, $30 to $35 million for the Marines, and $31 to $38 million for the Navy.

The way to meet this requirement is to ensure that each version just meets the individual service's needs, to make sure that the needs of one service do not result in the other versions being more costly or less effective, and to package the necessary differences ingeniously so that the benefits of commonality are preserved in production, training, and support.

Lockheed Martin's design flies the low-risk banner. Six months after the CDA source selection, Lockheed Martin had picked up both of the major partners in the defeated McDonnell Douglas team, as Northrop Grumman (with its carrier experience) and British Aerospace (and its STOVL knowledge) joined the X-35 program. The project is still being run by Lockheed Martin Tactical Aircraft Systems (LMTAS) at Fort Worth, but the prototypes are being built by the Skunk Works at Palmdale. Flight tests will start in 2000.

The X-35 is clearly a cousin to the F-22: the basic aerodynamics are similar, and the two aircraft take the same approach to stealth, with a combination of flat and curved surfaces and a sharp chine around the perimeter of the airframe. The main differences between the two aircraft (apart from size and the single engine) are the X-35's new "diverterless" inlet, with a bump on the inner wall rather than a splitter plate, and the axisymmetrical nozzle. Unlike the F-22, the X-35 does not use thrust vectoring in up-and-away flight.

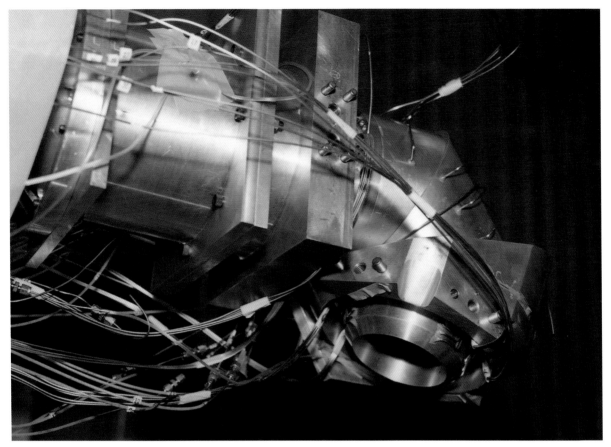

A test rig for the three-bearing exhaust nozzle. The cylindrical duct incorporates two tapered sections. These are connected to each other, the fixed exhaust and the final nozzle by three rotational bearings. The bearings rotate differentially to turn the final nozzle up to 110 degrees from the horizontal. The nozzle weighs less than a two-dimensional vectoring nozzle and is mechanically simple. Lockheed Martin

The JSF also lacks the larger F-22's "cheek" missile bays. Instead, it has two bays to the left and right of the keel, each with two doors. The inner door in each bay carries a launch rail for an AIM-120 AMRAAM. The outer door is slightly bulged on the Navy and Air Force versions to accommodate a 900-kilogram weapon. The wing includes four hard points, rated at 5,000 pounds (2,270 kilograms) inboard and 2,500 pounds (1,135 kilograms) outboard.

The STOVL version is externally identifiable by a slight bulge in the spine and a shorter canopy. The lift fan, developed by Allison Advanced Development Company (AADC), is located behind the cockpit in a bay with upper and lower clamshell doors. The lift fan supports almost half the airplane's weight in hovering flight, producing 18,000 pounds thrust (80 kiloNewtons). The lift fan doubles the mass flow of the propulsion system, and boosts its thrust by 44 percent.

Air from the engine fan feeds two roll control ducts that extend out to the wing fold line. The core exhaust flows through a three-bearing

A test version of the vented-D exhaust nozzle for the lift fan. The Lockheed Martin concept needs to vector the lift-fan thrust in order to accomplish STO and a smooth transition. The vented-D nozzle is made of vizor-like overlapping segments that extend below the aircraft, vectoring the thrust up to 90 degrees aft. Lockheed Martin

nozzle, developed by Rolls-Royce along the pattern of the Yak-141 exhaust. Another distinguishing feature of the STOVL version is an auxiliary inlet for the main engine, above the fuselage.

One of the key advantages of this system, compared to a direct-lift system such as the Harrier or Boeing X-32, is that pitch-and-roll control can be accomplished by modulating the thrust of the four lift posts, rather than by bleeding air (and power) from the engine to a dedicated control system. Valves in the roll ducts open and close differentially for roll control. In the pitch axis, energy can be switched between the

engine exhaust nozzle and the fan by adjusting the main engine's exhaust nozzle and the inlet guide vanes on the fan. Total thrust and efficiency remain unchanged.

As the Lockheed Martin design has evolved, the differences between the three variants have been accentuated. In the original concept, the different service variants were to be externally identical, out to the edges of the fixed-wing structure; the Navy version would have larger leading-edge and trailing-edge flaps, longer outer wings, and larger horizontal stabilizers.

Lockheed Martin now feels that its choice of a tail-aft design has been vindicated, because the designers have been able to provide the CV version with a much larger wing, while maintaining the same wing-body geometry. On a delta wing, any attempt to increase span will tend to lengthen or thicken the root or drive the designer to a lower sweep angle, which changes the wing's lift characteristics and may not match the center of gravity of the body.

Lockheed Martin's test plans reflect the order in which the company perceives technical risks. The greatest of these concerns STOVL propulsion and control; the next is the handling and control of the CV variant; and the lowest risks are in the up-and-away handling of the U.S. Air Force version. The first X-35 will initially be used for ground tests of the STOVL system, including "hover pit" and suspended testing. The STOVL components will then be removed and reinstalled in the second aircraft, which will continue into ground tests and make the first STOVL flights. Meanwhile, the first aircraft will be used for a short series

The lift fan on the Lockheed Martin JSF produces as much thrust as a small jetliner engine from two, counter-rotating fan stages. Variable inlet guide vanes control the mass of air through the fan, rapidly and responsively reducing its thrust. At the same time, the nozzle of the main engine opens and closes, adjusting the thrust of the rear lift post. This gives the fighter responsive control in pitch. Lockheed Martin

The drive system for the lift fan is mechanically simple. A spur gear on the drive shaft is located between a facing pair of bull gears—the lower of these is shown here—one of which drives each fan stage. This splits the torque, balances mechanical loads on the shaft, and drives both stages in opposite directions. A multiplate dry clutch with carbon pads, based on aircraft brake technology and operated by a digital control, engages the fan for landing and takeoff. Lockheed Martin

of CTOL tests before being modified into the CV version. Either aircraft can be modified to perform the entire range of tests, providing a back-up in the event of an accident.

The X-32 design with which Boeing entered the JSF contest was the direct result of studies started in 1992. From the outset, the company's goal was a low-cost, tri-service fighter with the highest possible degree of commonality.

Both cost and commonality persuaded Boeing to choose a direct-lift configuration, with no lift-augmenting devices such as a lift fan. Without a thrust post behind the cockpit, this meant that the main lift nozzles would have to be located on the center of gravity. In the interests of low cost and simplicity, Boeing's designers put the engine in the front of the airplane with vectoring nozzles behind it. The nozzles were used for take-off, transition,

and landing and were retracted in cruising flight. A long duct from the engine led to the augmentor and a pitch-axis vectoring nozzle in the tail.

Boeing's approach meant that the vertical landing weight was limited by the largest possible derivative engine: an F119 with a larger fan and increased bypass ratio. This, in turn, made it important to achieve the lowest possible empty weight, while providing enough internal fuel capacity and wing area to meet payload and range requirements. Consequently, Boeing selected a thick, structurally efficient, large-volume delta wing, with enough fuel capacity to make external fuel tanks almost superfluous.

Folding a delta wing is difficult because the fold joint is long and deep. Boeing recognized, however, that a delta could fit in the same deck spot as an F-18 without folding the wings, as long as the overall length was kept small. But with the engine in the front of the aircraft, conventional bifurcated inlets would add several feet to the overall length, so Boeing selected a radical forward-swept chin inlet.

The wing was set high on the body, to minimize "suck-down" effects. The jet exhausts tend to induce high-speed airflows under the wing, creating a low-pressure zone that tends to glue the aircraft to the ground. The upper and lower skins of the wing would be made in one piece, from a carbon-fiber composite material that uses a thermoplastic matrix.

The result was an aircraft in three main sections: the one-piece wing; the forebody, con-

Lockheed Martin's STOVL propulsion system started its test runs in early 1999 at Pratt and Whitney's West Palm Beach facility, the basic JSF119-611 engine having run in 1998. The lift fan casing is visible between and behind the large conical metal-mesh inlet covers, and the lift fan exhaust flows into the dumpster-like deflector beneath the fan. Testing was to establish the controllability and performance of the entire system. Pratt and Whitney

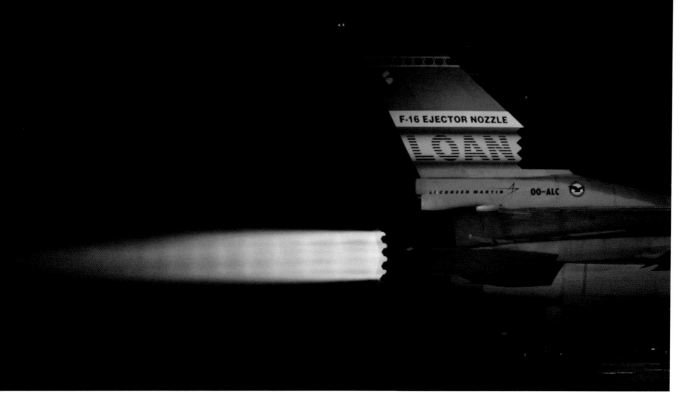

The Lockheed Martin JSF will have an exhaust nozzle that meets low-observable requirements at a lower weight and cost than the F-22's two-dimensional nozzle. This is Pratt and Whitney's low-observable, axisymmetrical nozzle (LOAN) under test on an F-16. Scalloped nozzle flaps control its radar reflectivity, and it incorporates an ejector system that mixes engine cooling air with the exhaust to reduce the infrared signature. Lockheed Martin

taining the cockpit and avionics; and the underwing nacelle, which accommodates the engine, powered-lift system, and weapon bays. Most of the components unique to the STOVL version are in the nacelle.

Boeing was highly confident of the merits of its design. Compared with the shaft-driven or gas-driven lift-fan approaches, it seemed simple and was likely to cost less to build and operate. The company's approach to commonality, confining differences to the smallest possible number of parts, made sense. The more that the JAST office stressed affordability, the more Boeing believed in its delta-wing design; and, unlike Lockheed Martin or McDonnell Douglas, Boeing did not fundamentally change its CALF design as it approached the CDA down-select.

The design clearly had changed in detail, however. Early Boeing impressions, the company's statements in 1993–94, and the company's patent applications show that the original design was a relatively small aircraft with an operating empty weight close to that of an F-16 (about 18,500 pounds or 8,400 kilograms), a near-stock F119 engine, and internal space for two AMRAAMs or other small weapons. The Boeing designers assumed that the future fighter would operate in conjunction with off-board sensors such as AWACS and Joint STARS radar surveillance aircraft, so that it would not need long-range sensors.

JAST called for a much larger internal weapons bay and a full suite of sensors, and the Navy's CV version was required to land aboard the carrier with a heavy weapon load.

Lockheed Martin's first X-35 prototype, near completion at Palmdale in June 1999. The lift-fan bay is clearly visible behind the cockpit. The company chose to have the Skunk Works build the first aircraft by traditional methods, and built large airframe assemblies in a parallel program to demonstrate low-cost manufacturing techniques. The two prototypes are basically similar, and "picture-frame" assemblies will be fitted around the basic wing-box to demonstrate the Navy configuration. Lockheed Martin

This drove the size and thrust upward. The wingtip fins were moved to the aft fuselage, and the U.S. Air Force and Navy versions acquired extended wingtips.

In aircraft design, the goal is to meet the user's requirements in a single configuration at the lowest possible weight and cost. As the designers put it, the configuration converges on an optimum. But if a given layout cannot be made to meet all the requirements and fails to converge, there is no choice but to modify it radically and start again.

Around the end of 1997, it became clear that Boeing's delta JSF design was not converging. It appears that the CV version's approach performance, and handling were marginal, but (unlike Lockheed Martin) Boeing could not easily make the wing bigger. The wing was already as big as the body could accommodate. Even so, the demands of the CV

mission had increased the weight to the point where the largest practical version of the F119 would barely allow the STOVL version to land vertically with the desired weapon load.

The JSF designers in Seattle and their former rivals in St. Louis worked during the first half of 1998 on two designs: an improved delta and a swept-wing aircraft with a horizontal tail. The latter was selected as the basis for the PWSC design in the fall of 1998, although it was not revealed in public until early 1999.

Boeing's best friends could not argue that the change improved the fighter's looks. Neither did it improve the company's chances in the contest. The purpose of building the CDA prototypes is to demonstrate novel, critical features of the JSF designs at full scale. As far as the operators are concerned, two of these demonstrations—STOVL tests and the CV approach test—are paramount.

Boeing's original JSF design, used in the X-32 CDA aircraft, was a pure delta with no horizontal tail. Most of the structural loads were carried in a one-piece wing. Eventually, the weight of the trailing-edge control actuators grew to the point where a tail was a lighter solution. Boeing

Boeing's X-32 will have the same STOVL powered-lift system as the EMD design, but the EMD version will have different characteristics in transition because it will have greater pitch-and-roll authority. In the case of the CV version, X-32 tests will be almost irrelevant.

The Boeing inlet is also considered a high-risk area of the design. Because the engine is installed far forward, the inlet has a sharp S-curve and changes from a polygonal to a circular cross-section in a short distance. Boeing will have to demonstrate that the significant difference in shape between the CDA and EMD inlets does not imply any risks in transition to EMD.

Boeing has spread the CDA program across the newly expanded company. The Boeing X-32

CDAs are being assembled, checked out, and tested from a former Rockwell facility at Palmdale, California, next door to the Lockheed Martin Skunk Works. The old Boeing had no fast-jet flight-test facility, and some tests will be conducted at Edwards Air Force Base, minutes away from Palmdale. The forward fuselage assemblies, including the cockpit, will be designed and built at the Phantom Works in St. Louis. St. Louis is responsible for the STOVL portion of the flight control laws.

Construction of the CDA prototypes is only part of the JSF project. Pratt and Whitney has a demanding role in the CDA program. The challenge is to flight-qualify four distinct propulsion systems—STOVL and

Boeing's X-32A demonstrator retains the original delta design. Either of the two CDA aircraft can be modified to perform all the CDA tests, providing back-up in the event of an accident. The canopy is from an AV-8B. Boeing

CTOL propulsion for two designs—in three years. In 1998, Pratt and Whitney started tests of the JSF prototype engines, the JSF 119-PW-611 for the Lockheed X-35 and the JSF 119-PW-614 for the X-32.

For Boeing, Pratt and Whitney provides the entire propulsion and reaction control system, with the exception of the Rolls-Royce–developed lift module, the exhaust section immediately aft of the engine which incorporates the retractable vectoring nozzle. In the Lockheed Martin design, Rolls-Royce provides the final nozzle of the STOVL variant and Allison supplies the lift fan and its drive system.

The Boeing engine is the most powerful fighter engine ever designed, believed to produce a thrust in excess of 40,000 pounds (180 kilo-Newtons) without augmentation. It combines the modified F119 core with a scaled-up F119 fan and a new, two-stage, low-pressure turbine. The Lockheed Martin engine's fan is midway in size between the F119 and Boeing fans, but there is still a larger LP turbine to drive the lift fan. Both CDA engines produce more power than the standard F119 and have been modified as necessary with new materials coatings so that they can run at higher temperatures.

Pratt and Whitney is also working on the design of the production engine. The JSF

Boeing JSF Propulsion Concept (STOVL)

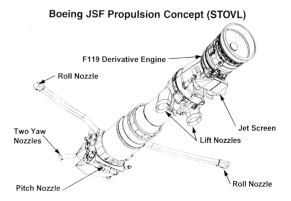

The Boeing powered-lift system is completely different from Lockheed's. In the STOVL mode, the two-dimensional thrust-vectoring nozzle is designed to close off the main exhaust. At the same time, butterfly valves direct the exhaust through vectoring nozzles. The roll, pitch, and yaw nozzles are fed from the rear of the extended exhaust duct, and a wide, narrow "jet screen" nozzle under the forward fuselage, fed with engine bleed air, both helps to balance the aircraft and to prevent exhaust gas from being ingested into the engine. Pratt and Whitney

engine will resemble the F119 in most respects, but will be very different in one characteristic: cost. The target cost for the JSF engine, one engineer remarks, is "not even close" to the F119. On the production JSF engine, Pratt and Whitney has already decided to replace some of the composites in the F119-PW-100 with heavier but less costly metal and to use solid fan blades in place of hollow titanium components.

Another new feature of the JSF engine will be a "prognostic" feature built into its control system, intended to predict failures before they damage the engine or imperil the aircraft. This will comprise sensors that monitor pressures, temperatures, vibration, and stresses in the engine and sample the exhaust stream for metal particles. Combined with a computer model of the engine and with a detailed history of its use, this should allow the prognostic system to identify signs of incipient failures.

Despite Pratt and Whitney's optimism that the JSF 119 engine will be up to its task, the JSF program office is making sure that there will be an alternative engine, developed by a General Electric/Allison/Rolls-Royce team. General Electric has been heading the design of the YF120-FX engine since 1996.

The YF120-FX core should be tested in mid-2000, and a complete engine should be ground-tested in 2001. EMD should start in 2003, and the alternate engine should be available in Lot 4 for delivery in 2010. Pratt and Whitney's JSF engine will be the only engine available on the first 100 or so aircraft; after that, the Pentagon's JSF engine buy will be split each year, with the size of each supplier's share determined by an annual competition. New export customers will be able to choose either engine.

If the Pentagon thinks that commonality is so important for JSF, why are there two engines? One reason is that memories of the Pratt and Whitney F100 engine, which was developed for the F-15 and F-16, are fresh enough to hurt. The F100 suffered from nagging problems, which were not fixed until the U.S. Air Force commissioned the General Electric F110 as an alternative engine. The JSF is also uniquely vulnerable to engine problems. Reliability and performance cannot be traded against one another: A shortfall in performance or handling could render the STOVL version unworkable, while a reliability problem would be unacceptable to the U.S. Navy.

While the JSF will not set any new records in weapon load, speed, agility, and range, it will, in many respects, be very unusual under the skin. Structures, subsystems, and avionics have all been reinvented. The common factor in all these areas is to save money. Although joint production will help reduce costs, the battle to meet the cost targets will be won or lost on the details.

One of the biggest such challenges will be achieving low-cost stealth. Although details are

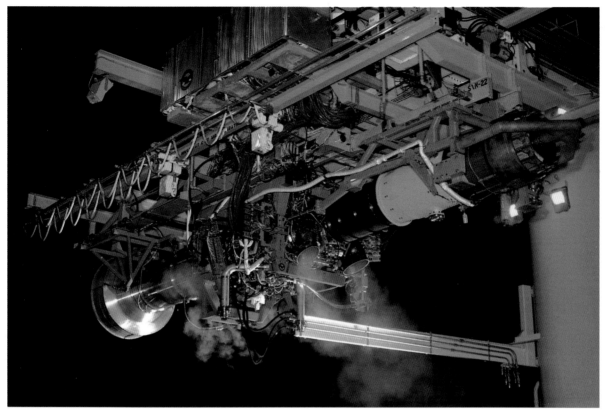

Boeing's propulsion system under test at West Palm Beach, on Pratt and Whitney's outdoor test stand. The inlet is on the left, the vectoring nozzles are visible in the center, and a gas stream from the forward "jet screen" nozzle can be seen to the left of the main nozzles. The two-dimensional aft nozzle, which incorporates the yaw-and-roll control off-takes, has not yet been installed. Pratt and Whitney

veiled by national and competitive security concerns, the JSF is likely to follow the approach taken by the F-22's designers, who have attempted to reduce the high maintenance costs associated with stealth on earlier aircraft.

The main challenge in stealth maintenance is dealing with gaps and openings in the skin. Unless a gap is properly sealed, it will interrupt the flow of electromagnetic energy over the skin and cause unwanted and unpredictable radar reflections. The first key to affordable stealth, therefore, is to minimize the number of openings and gaps.

For example, one important thrust in the JSF avionics system is to use shared electronic and optical sensor apertures. In the radio-frequency (RF) band, a total of just over 20 antennas should replace almost 60 antennas on the F-22, covering communications, navigation, and identification functions with passive and active surveillance, while a common set of IR sensors performs targeting, navigation, and threat warning functions. This eliminates 40 specially designed and treated antenna mountings.

Structurally, the use of large, integrated composite parts will eliminate skin gaps and fasteners, and the JSF will make the greatest possible use of the weapon bays and landing

The original Boeing JSF is shown completing its transition after a ski-jump STO from an Invincible-class carrier. Developed by Rolls-Royce, the powered-lift nozzles move from the vertical through the straight-aft position and into a stowage position in one rotating movement. The aircraft is flying on its wings before the aft nozzle opens. Boeing

gear bay doors to provide access to the most frequently maintained systems.

Where an access panel is needed, a stealth designer has a choice between two types of access panel. A conventional panel is light and inexpensive, but has to be sealed with tape, caulk, or putty after it is removed. Engineers call this "breaking the LO bubble"; after the panel is reinstalled, the seal has to be checked to make sure that the airplane is still stealthy.

The alternative is a frequent access panel, which can be opened and closed easily; however, it must be rigid and fitted with a secure latching system and a special gasket so that it will not cause a physical or electromagnetic discontinuity in the surface when it is closed.

On a stealth aircraft, it is also worth investing time and money to make sure that internal components do not need frequent maintenance. On the YF-22 prototype, Lockheed engineers made a point of measuring the heat and vibration levels inside the structure. Internal components—from pipes to pumps to computers—are designed to withstand the real environment rather than to a standard military specification. Another important tool for LO support is diagnostics—knowing exactly what broke, so the maintainer knows which panel to take off.

There does not appear to have been any revolutionary advances in radar absorbent material (RAM) since the early days of stealth, although there has been steady progress in creating materials that are effective but robust and easy to repair. Like the F-22, JSF will use fewer kinds of LO material than the B-2 and F-117, where LO goals were paramount and designers tended to select the material best suited to the requirements in any particular location, with the result that different types of material proliferated.

Further complicating JSF's stealth requirements is the fact that the aircraft is intended to be exported. The Pentagon's first idea was that export JSFs—with the exception of the United Kingdom aircraft—would be delivered without secret LO materials. There were several problems with this approach. Simply removing RAM would produce an aircraft with LO characteristics that would be unpredictable, which is to say useless. Developing a JSF variant with higher, fully modeled radar cross-section levels than the standard U.S. aircraft would be expensive and raised more questions. Would the export version need an active electronic jammer (unlike the standard model)? Was it worth giving up maneuverability and AIM-9 capability for a reduced level of stealth?

By late 1998, the commanders-in-chief (CINCs) in charge of U.S. forces around the world had weighed into the debate. Coalition operations, they argued, would be almost impossible if different partners in the force had JSFs with different stealth characteristics. In early 1999, this argument appeared to

This is a model of the Boeing JSF in vertical landing mode. The powered-lift system is basically unchanged in the company's new configuration. In jet-borne flight, a rapidly rising "fountain" of hot air forms between the twin vertical exhaust streams where they strike the ground. The cover doors for the powered-lift nozzles and the forward jet-screen nozzle, combined with retractable under-fuselage dams, trap this fountain and add to the vertical lift. Bill Sweetman

The original Boeing JSF, in its Royal Navy STOVL version, had a notably short clipped delta wing. Leading-edge and trailing-edge flaps would be drooped to increase lift. Bill Sweetman

The STOVL version of the Boeing aircraft, shown in Marine Corps trim with extended wingtips (and, fancifully, two F4U Corsairs in formation). The JSF requirement calls for four external pylons, which can be used for drop tanks, large stand-off weapons such as JASSM or the High Speed Anti-Radiation Missile, or additional AAMs. Boeing

have won the day, and the JSF office is looking for ways in which non-U.S. customers can operate fully capable JSFs without compromising their technology.

Nobody quite knows how to do this yet. Getting as close as possible to zero-maintenance stealth (so that non-U.S. maintenance crews do not repair and remove materials and coatings) is a start. If LO-treated parts are damaged, they could be replaced on the flight line and returned to the United States for

repair. Probably, a combination of security measures will be required.

Internally, JSF will pioneer another major change in technology, which stems indirectly from work under the Star Wars program in the 1980s. Looking at the need to put powerful electrical systems on spacecraft, Star Wars researchers developed new ways of converting and controlling electrical power in lightweight, solid-state packages. This technology now makes it practical to use electrical power

To provide the high lift required for a carrier approach, Boeing modified its CV version with vortex flaps above the inner wing leading edges. Hinged on their aft edge, these surfaces would open up to a 45-degree angle, trapping the leading edge vortex and boosting lift on the apex of the wing. The trailing-edge elevons drooped to trim the aircraft, allowing the wing to reach the lift coefficient required for a carrier approach without the high angle of attack that has generally made tailless deltas unsuitable for carrier use. Another unique feature of the CV version was the nose landing gear: Unable to stow the required twin-wheel unit beneath the inlet duct, the Boeing engineers created a split gear that placed the wheels on either side of the duct. Boeing

to replace the high-pressure hydraulic systems that move the airplane's flight controls, landing gear, and other components. Electrical wiring requires less maintenance than hydraulic lines and is less vulnerable to combat damage.

The U.S. Air Force was working on this technology before JSF started and had concluded that the logical extension was to develop an integrated system that would replace all the mechanical accessories normally connected to the fighter's engine. This effort was absorbed by JSF and is now known as JSF Integrated Subsystems Technology (J/IST).

J/IST demonstration contracts are shared between the two teams, and the results are

available to both sides. Lockheed Martin is leading the in-flight demonstration of electric technology and is modifying the hard-worked Advanced Fighter Technology Integration (AFTI) F-16 prototype as the first fighter to fly with all its primary flight controls both signaled and powered by electricity, and with no mechanical backup.

Under development by Boeing, the other element of J/IST replaces a number of complex systems in today's fighters. A modern fighter engine has a tower shaft that links the high-pressure spool of the engine to an airframe-mounted accessory drive (AMAD). The AMAD is a compact package of gears, clutches, and constant-speed drives that, in turn, drives the

One of Boeing's goals in its JSF design was to reduce the total number of air frame parts by designing large one-piece structures. This one-piece wing skin was made from carbon fibers in a thermoplastic matrix. Thermoplastic materials can be heated and reset, unlike the thermoset resins in most composite structures, and they are tough and resistant to damage. The technology has not matured as fast as expected, however, and Boeing is proposing a carbon-fiber/thermoset wing for the production JSF. *Boeing*

hydraulic pumps, electrical generators, and the environmental control system (ECS) compressor. A gas-turbine auxiliary power unit (APU) or an emergency power unit may also be connected to the AMAD to start the engine and to power essential systems when the engine is not running.

The core of the J/IST system is the thermal and energy management module (T/EMM), produced by AlliedSignal. This has three components on a single shaft: a cooling turbine that circulates air through the primary ECS cooling loop; a 270-volt DC electric starter/generator, which is the aircraft's secondary electrical power source and starts the T/EMM; and a power turbine, which is normally driven by engine bleed air and also incorporates a small combustor. The engine's tower shaft is connected to a second starter/generator, and there is no mechanical connection between the engine and the T/EMM.

In normal operation, the engine-mounted generator provides all secondary power for the aircraft, providing electrical power to the flight controls. Hydraulic systems may still be used in some areas (such as brakes and doors), but they will be small zonal systems powered by electric pumps. Bleed air from the engine drives the T/EMM, which provides ECS air.

If the engine-mounted generator fails, the combustor is activated, giving the T/EMM extra power to run its own generator and the ECS. The combustor mode can be used to start the engine on the ground. The T/EMM also incorporates a stored-air system to provide emergency power if the main engine stops at high altitude and low airspeed. Compressed air from a storage reservoir spins the T/EMM turbine, generating enough electrical power to keep the aircraft under control as the pilot dives into thicker air where an air-start is possible.

Another new feature of J/IST is that the ram-air heat exchangers that cool the air in the ECS loop, extracting the heat produced by the electronics, are located in the main engine fan duct, while the T/EMM power turbine exhaust is dumped into the main exhaust nozzle. This eliminates the radar and infrared

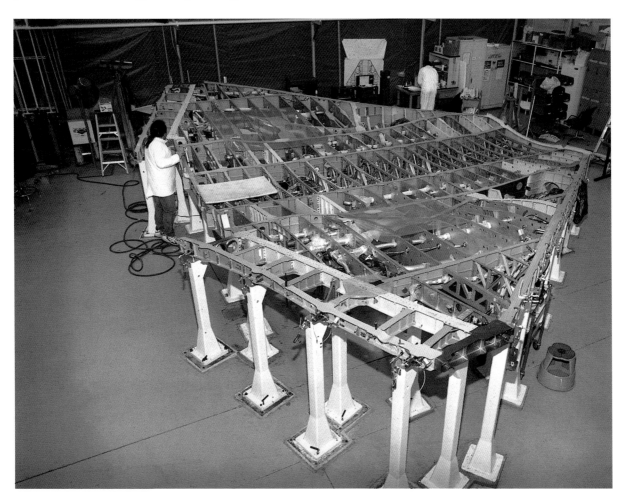

The depth of the delta wing is apparent in this view of the X-32 structure under assembly. The ability to carry a great deal of fuel in the wing is a key to the Boeing design approach. Boeing

Boeing used fiber placement technology to build complex parts for the X-32s, such as this one-piece inlet duct assembly. Fiber placement is an automated process in which a narrow band of continuous carbon-fiber "tow" is laid up around a male form or mandrel in a precise, computer-defined pattern. It allows complex parts with compound curvature to be produced in one piece. Boeing

signatures of the ECS and APU inlets and exhausts, which otherwise have to be screened or protected by doors. The ECS incorporates a gas separator, which produces oxygen for the pilot, gaseous nitrogen to inert the fuel tanks, and liquid nitrogen to cool thermal sensors.

JSF will also use new structural technology to reduce both weight and cost—a radical change from earlier advanced composite materials, which saved some weight but cost the earth to produce. Boeing's Phantom Works, under the Advanced Lightweight Aircraft Fuselage Structure (ALAFS) program, is building a complete F/A-18E center-section using new techniques. The aim is to reduce the weight of aircraft structure by 20 percent,

Boeing's first X-32 is structurally complete at Palmdale in June 1999. In this view, it is very apparent that the cockpit perches above the very large inlet, and that the wing unites the forebody and nacelle. The vertical tails and landing gear have been installed, but the translating inlet cowl has not been fitted yet. Boeing

compared with conventional aluminum and titanium construction, while reducing life-cycle costs by 30 percent. ALAFS uses fiber-placement techniques to build up composite skins, rather than time-consuming fabric lay-ups. Components that would usually have been made from many sheet metal parts and innumerable fasteners are produced by high-speed machining. Resin-transfer molding is used for wing spars.

The tools and materials that are used to build an airplane are only half the cost battle, though. The cost of building and assembling an aircraft is built into every part and the way in which it is designed. Lockheed Martin is working with IBM and Dassault to expand Dassault's CATIA computer-aided design system into a "virtual development environment." The goal is 100 percent digital prototyping: As the designer works on a component, the effects

The new swept-wing version of the Boeing JSF retains the basic construction of the original, with a thick one-piece wing and a straight-sided fuselage beneath it. A lighter, raked-back inlet has replaced the characteristic yawning-hippo inlet of the X-32. The small horizontal tails improve both pitch-and-roll control, because more of the trailing-edge surface can now be used to provide roll authority. Boeing

of a design decision on part manufacture, assembly, and support are simulated on the computer before any physical work is done. By simulating all these effects, it is possible to calculate the impact of a design decision on life-cycle cost.

Advanced CAD techniques are key to building three distinct JSF versions on the same production line. The designer's dilemma is that each version encounters different structural loads. If the airframes are identical, and all parts are strong enough to take the load imposed by the heaviest version, the other variants will be too heavy. On the other hand, if the aircraft are different, the benefits of commonality are lost.

An early Boeing study, based on CAD techniques, introduced the concept of "cousin

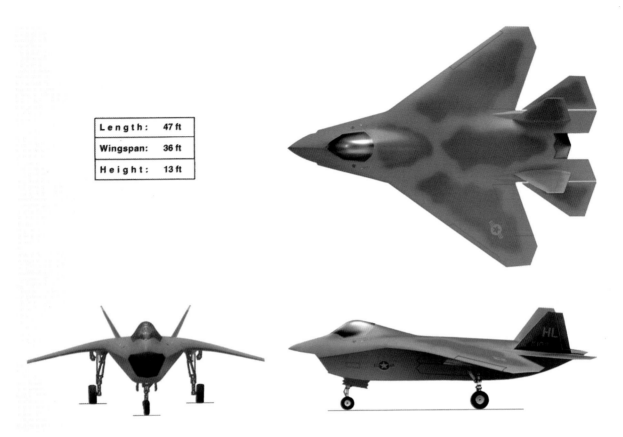

Length:	47 ft
Wingspan:	36 ft
Height:	13 ft

Despite the addition of tails to the Boeing design, the overall length has been kept short, so that the Navy version does not need a folding wing. The cockpit is located directly above the inlet duct and the nose landing gear bay, and the back of the pilot's seat is just in front of the engine face. Boeing

parts." These might, for example, be components that carry more load on the Navy version than they do on the Marine Corps and Air Force aircraft, but are otherwise unaffected by the different missions. Cousin parts differ in thickness, weight, and strength but are built on the same tools, with the same materials and are assembled in the same way. Because there are three JSF versions, every component falls into one of five groups: tri-common (common on three versions), dual-common, tri-cousin, dual-cousin, and unique. CAD allows the designer to try a series of different combinations of common, cousin, and unique parts and to evaluate which combination is most economical.

Avionics account for as much as a third of the cost of a fighter, so the JSF cost goals give the contractors no option but to find ways to make electronic systems less costly. This is a competitive and generally guarded area of the JSF program, and relatively little new information has been released since the competition started.

Broadly speaking, the JSF goal is to take the capabilities of the F-22, add air-to-surface capability, and subtract a lot of weight and a lot of money. Like the F-22, the JSF will have a centralized system in which most avionics functions (such as mission management and signal processing) reside in an Integrated Core Processor (ICP), a powerful battery of

Boeing has rearranged the STOVL version's reaction control system, adding two forward nozzles, fed by engine bleed air, to increase pitch authority. The roll-control ducts have been extended to match the repositioned wing trailing edge. The translating inlet of the original design is still used, although its shape has changed. Boeing

computers. As on the F-22, the ICP is likely to have a back plane providing power, cooling, and data connections to easily changed snap-in modules.

The main difference will be an emphasis on an open architecture and the use of commercial standards. The goal is to design the ICP so that the modules can use whatever processors the commercial market can supply, as JSFs are built and upgraded. Not only are these commercial chips likely to be cheaper and higher-performing than a custom chip, but a chip developed today for JSF may not even be available in 2008.

As on the F-22, the JSF sensors are apertures that act as peripherals to the ICP, which will fuse sensor information and off-board data with database information before feeding it to the displays.

One of the most important programs in this area is the Multi-Function Integrated Radio Frequency System (MIRFS). Raytheon (formerly Hughes) and Northrop Grumman (formerly

Boeing's design changes were driven in large measure by an increase in the Navy's required bring-back weapon load, combined with tougher requirements for approach speed. The Navy version of the Boeing JSF features ailerons as well as the large flaperons that are used on the other two variants. Boeing

The U.S. Air Force and Navy variants of the Boeing JSF each carry some 16,000 pounds of internal fuel, most of it in the broad one-piece wing. This is close to twice the internal fuel capacity of comparable-sized fighters today and almost eliminates the need for external fuel tanks for most missions. Boeing

Westinghouse) have been under contract to develop MIRFS since early 1996. MIRFS is a forward-looking active array (that is, a mechanically fixed array comprising many small transmit/receive modules), which will operate over a large band width both as a conventional radar and as a highly sensitive, directionally accurate receiver. MIRFS is due to fly before 2000.

The JSF program office envisages a wideband, all-aspect RF system, using high-performance shared antennas. A single antenna will be used to pick up intraflight data-link signals, long-range transmissions, and enemy sensors over a wide band. Some of these antennas will be of the "smart-skin" type, embedded directly in the aircraft's skin rather

than being placed in complex treated cavities.

The electro-optical system will likewise use high-performance apertures to perform many different functions. The JSF will have high-resolution, solid-state infrared focal plane arrays built into the nose, tail, and body sides. Covering a complete globe around the vehicle, they will combine the function of a missile launch warning system, a long-range infrared search-and-track system, and an imaging IR system.

Like the F-22, the JSF will carry a high-band width, low-probability-of-intercept datalink, which will allow each aircraft in a formation to use and display sensor data from any of the other aircraft. Tactically, this opens up interesting options. One aircraft, for example,

One new technology being developed with JSF in mind is the use of appliqués in place of paint or radar-absorbent coatings, shown here under test on an F-16. Lockheed Martin and 3M have experimented with these polymer materials, which are attached to the structure with strong but readily removable adhesives. Precut sheets are used to cover large surfaces, and formed "boots" are used for wing and tail edges. A major advantage of appliqué coatings is that they are easier to repair than a painted surface, particularly on a carrier at sea. Lockheed Martin

can act as a mini-AWACS for the group, using its radar to track targets, while the others can fire and guide AMRAAMs in radar silence. Alternatively, the operator need not fit all the aircraft in a fleet with a complete avionics suite, reducing costs; or a JSF could be launched with an equipment failure that would normally keep it on the ground, improving availability.

The main innovation in the JSF cockpit is that the most important display may be a wide-field-of-view, binocular helmet-mounted display (HMD) capable of presenting imagery. In fact, the Lockheed Martin JSF mock-up has no head-up display. The HMD is the primary display for navigation, flight control, and weapon aiming. The HMD can present either real or synthetic imagery. For example, if the aircraft is flying at low altitude in rain or cloud, the on-board terrain database could produce a synthetic picture of the terrain to help the pilot maintain orientation.

Both JSF teams are developing their avionics systems in ground laboratories, simulators, and flying test beds. Lockheed Martin is using Northrop Grumman's long-serving BAC One-Eleven, and Boeing has modified a 737. Both aircraft feature representative sensors, processors, and a mock-up cockpit.

What is most significant about this Lockheed Martin JSF cockpit mock-up is what is not there: The head-up display, a fixture of the fighter cockpit since the late 1960s, is missing. Instead, the pilot has a binocular, full-color helmet-mounted display (HMD), capable of showing data, target location, and IR or synthetic imagery in any direction. The HMD is also a targeting device; combined with GPS and a terrain database on the aircraft, the pilot can designate a target for a guided weapon simply by looking at it and selecting it with an HMD cursor. One advantage of removing the HUD is that its optical system no longer resides behind the upper central part of the instrument panel. This allows the central large-format color displays to be made larger and moved upward into the pilot's field of view. Lockheed Martin

Lockheed Martin's automated design and engineering system is based on Dassault's CATIA. It includes knowledge-based "design checkers" that automatically search for problems and unwanted interactions between components. It also uses common visualization tools. In an early-1997 demonstration, it was already possible to "fly through" the JSF production line and steer the observation point into small details of the assembly. Virtual mannequins can be seen assembling the aircraft, with different colors on their muscles to show much strain they are putting on their joints. Lockheed Martin

Whichever team wins JSF, the project has already done a great deal to focus attention on how to build combat aircraft at lower cost without sacrificing efficiency. Key technologies such as simpler composite structures, integrated power subsystems, and commercial-based avionics are being brought to maturity much faster in the JSF program than they might be otherwise. Three thousand aircraft are a juicy carrot; being excluded from the Pentagon market for a generation is a threatening stick. In fact, there is a good chance that history will remember JSF for that, more than anything else.

Boeing will modify this Boeing 737 as a test-bed for the JSF avionics, with a representative set of electronic and optical sensors and a crew station. Boeing

4

INTO THE WILD PURPLE YONDER

As these words are written, in early 1999, the official policy in the Pentagon is that 3,000-plus JSFs will be produced and the EMD decision will take place in early 2001. This will not happen.

The cardinal requirements for JSF have been defined by the need to sustain the existing force structure. For the Navy, the critical need is to provide its carriers with a long-range, stealthy strike aircraft. Without it, even the massive USS Stennis (named after the senator who helped kill the controversial Sea Control Ship V/STOL carrier in the 1970s) will be unable to reach targets much more than 200 miles inland or to tackle heavy air defenses. Newport News

A new U.S. administration will be elected in November 2000. Replacing a two-term administration is no small affair, even if current Vice President Al Gore succeeds Bill Clinton. Until the new civilian leaders at the Pentagon have found their offices (the incoming Clinton administration, in 1993, did not fill all its positions until well into the summer), they will not approve a program that will tie up much of the research-and-development budget for two full terms. They will not only review JSF, but they will look at U.S. military plans at the strategic level (under current plans, a second Quadrennial Defense Review is due in 2001).

The reviewers will almost certainly confront the fact that the JSF cannot be built at the original flyaway price points set in 1996. Set before the EMD aircraft had entered the preliminary design phase, these were educated guesses, bounded by projected budgets and the services' desired force structure.

The challenges faced by Boeing and Lockheed Martin in early 1999 are a warning sign. Boeing's delta-wing design acknowledged the need for simplicity to reduce costs, but it proved technically unable to meet the requirement. Lockheed Martin was, less visibly, working hard to demonstrate that its design, although it met the performance requirements, could be produced within sight of the original cost goal.

It is most unlikely that the contractors will be able to offer a fixed price for development. The only way to get near the JSF unit price targets is to incorporate new technologies: commercial, off-the-shelf avionics, integrated subsystems, electric actuation, and integrated design and manufacturing, for

After 2010, the Navy's air wings will move toward a mix of JSFs and the F/A-18E/F Super Hornet. In early 1999, reports suggested that the Super Hornet's range and air-combat performance were turning out to be disappointing. If so, JSF will become even more important to the future of Navy air power. Northrop Grumman

For the U.S. Air Force, the inexpensive alternative to the JSF is an improved F-16 such as the Block 60, selected in 1998 by the United Arab Emirates. With an electronically scanned radar, internal IR, and laser-designation system, and extra fuel in conformal tanks, the advanced F-16 is comparable to the JSF in most respects except stealth. If JSF is terminated or substantially delayed, the Air Force could well buy Block 60s. Lockheed Martin

example. But all of these are still at the stage of large-scale demonstrations or flying-laboratory work, and there will be open cost and technical risks when EMD begins.

Then there is the stealth issue: The current goal is to achieve ultra-low-maintenance stealth in a form that protects sensitive technology while permitting the vehicle itself to be exported. Nobody knows how to do that, let alone how much it will cost, and (once again) work will be at an early stage in 2001.

In any event, a fixed price at the start of EMD will be an outlandish fiction. A contractor wins JSF on a fixed-price offer, and its rival quits the fighter business. Four years later, the winner discloses that it cannot build the aircraft for that money. If the Pentagon enforces the contract, it will drive its only surviving fighter supplier into bankruptcy.

The reason for the low-cost target was a fundamental premise of the JSF program: that the force structure of 1993–94, when it

Lockheed Martin's AGM-158 Joint Air-to-Surface Standoff Missile (JASSM) represents a potential shift in deep-strike operations. Less expensive than most of today's cruise missiles, and carrying a larger warhead and a precision seeker, JASSM will be effective against many targets that cannot be reached today except by manned aircraft. Lockheed Martin

was designed, should change as little as possible: a U.S. Air Force fighter force of 20 to 22 wings, a 12-carrier Navy, and an independent Marine Corps air arm. Given the budgets projected in the mid-1990s, JSF could be seen as the only way to do this. In 2001, however, priorities may look different. Should the carriers be reassigned to support the Marines? Does the multirole fighter still form the linchpin of the Air Force, or are fewer, longer range platforms needed?

The Pentagon is looking at completely new weapons and concepts of warfare. Defense against missiles is a looming challenge and is driving the development of new missiles, reconnaissance and surveillance systems, and airborne lasers.

The U.S. Air Force is defining a new military space plane, to protect critical U.S. space assets, prevent other countries from using space-based assets against U.S. interests, and deliver precision-guided weapons over global ranges within minutes of launch. Early in 1999, the service announced a wholesale shift of research funds from aeronautics to space. When the astute Gen. George Muellner retired in 1998 and joined Boeing, he turned up neither in Seattle nor in St. Louis, but at

Increasingly, aircraft such as JSF will operate with the help of off-board sensors, such as the E-8C Joint STARS. With its long-range, high-resolution ground surveillance radar and team of onboard operators, Joint STARS can track individual targets while maintaining "big picture" surveillance of a wide area. The fighter will also be able to tap into information from any other sensor in the "battlespace"—from RAH-66 Comanche helicopters to reconnaissance UAVs and even satellites. It may launch weapons such as JASSM against targets that are not in view of its own sensors. Northrop Grumman

the company's advanced space launch headquarters in Seal Beach, California.

The whole question of whether and where the United States should maintain permanent overseas bases is being studied, in the wake of terrorist attacks on U.S. bases and embassies. One idea is to construct immense floating mobile operating bases (MOBs) capable of handling C-130s.

If these radical ideas are funded, the money will have to come from somewhere; and even if the 2001 strategic review confirms the need for a new tactical aircraft, the next question is whether JSF is the right solution for the 21st century. Modern as it is in some ways, JSF represents a traditional approach to fighter design, and there are technologies very close to hand that could change some basic assumptions.

JSF is based on the use of the low-cost JDAM-guided bomb to replace unguided munitions. Although JDAM has a state-of-the-art guidance system, the munition itself is a low-drag weapon from the 1950s, basically no different from a World War II bomb. In 1996–97, Air Force and Boeing researchers demonstrated that a 250-pound (114-kilogram) weapon, using precision guidance, modern fusing technology, and other features, could destroy many of the targets that would normally be attacked by a 2,000-pound (900-kilogram) JDAM.

Another premise behind JSF is that the air commander needs stealthy platforms to threaten a large number of defended, hardened targets with accurate but inexpensive weapons. Precision, long-range cruise missiles are too expensive to cover everything. The advent of the new AGM-158 Joint Air-to-Surface Stand-off Missile (JASSM) may change that equation. The $400,000 JASSM packs a 1,000-pound warhead and a precision guidance system and has a range in excess of 100 nautical miles (185 kilometers). It does not eliminate the need for manned aircraft and JDAMs, but it can take on a large part of the target set, which, today, cannot be attacked without a stealthy, manned platform. The result is that fewer such aircraft may be needed.

For attacks against SAM sites, PGMs, and armored vehicles, future fighters may deploy a new generation of "brilliant" munitions. Lockheed Martin's Low-Cost Autonomous Attack System (LOCAAS) is an example. Practicable wholly as a result of computer technology, LOCAAS is a 93-pound (42-kilogram), 100-nautical mile (180-kilogram) range vehicle capable of detecting and destroying vehicle targets within a preprogrammed area.

The LOCAAS air vehicle is 24 inches (0.76 meter) long and is powered by a tiny jet engine. It has a GPS/inertial navigation sys-tem and a lidar (laser radar) seeker and is armed with an explosively formed penetrator (EFP) warhead. Program officials claim that the lidar seeker can discriminate between different types of tanks, as well as discriminating trucks from tanks or SAM launchers. This allows the weapon to fire its warhead as a slug, a rod, or as fragments, depending on the target. The developers' goal is to start EMD in 2002 and achieve a limited operational capability in 2003.

Like AGM-158, LOCAAS could affect the requirements for the platforms that support it. The weapon is autonomous and relatively unlikely to cause collateral damage, so it does not have to be launched from an expensive, manned, multisensor platform.

Avionics are also on the cusp of a major change, pioneered by the F-22's intraflight datalink. If datalinks can be made reliable (granted, a large "if") and routine, then every airplane, helicopter, UAV, tank, and even soldier in the battle area, and the spacecraft above it, becomes part of a vast military Internet. Already, simple information systems allow a ground observer, with a hand-held range finder and GPS, to direct a pilot to attack a target that could never be acquired visually or with the airplane's own radar. The question Boeing raised in its early-1990s light fighter studies—whether every fighter needs its own autonomous long-range sensors—is not going to disappear.

Does every fighter need a pilot? Uninhabited combat air vehicles (UCAVs) popped into public view in 1996. They present some major challenges, but could play a role in dangerous missions (such as SEAD) or tedious missions (such as armed surveillance) by 2010 to 2015. A UCAV might, for example, be the best way to dispense LOCAAS.

Aircraft technology is not standing still. Under various programs, many of them classified, the Pentagon is believed to have worked on even stealthier platforms, combining very low RCS (significantly, most of the major players upgraded their test ranges in the 1990s to make them more sensitive) with infrared and visual stealth. Ultrastealthy aircraft would be expensive but would be able to take on the toughest targets without support, reducing the total number of aircraft needed to destroy a given set of targets.

Tailless configurations are one way to achieve lower levels of stealth, particularly from the side aspect, and also promise to reduce weight and drag. The Boeing X-36 has demonstrated one tailless configuration, with a combination of aerodynamic controls, canards, and vectored thrust; Lockheed Martin has proposed a delta-winged tailless demonstrator based on the F-16. As one veteran designer grumbles, looking at the X-35: "It's got at least four too many tail surfaces."

Even the jet engine, after 60 years of development, has a great deal of potential for improvement left. In 1987, the Pentagon launched a program with the tongue-twisting name of Integrated High Performance Turbine Engine Technology (IHPTET).

IHPTET was set up to pool the three principal services' resources in the development of all kinds of turbine engines and give them a set of simple long-term goals. The goals were to be achieved in three phases, with the intention that, as each phase was completed, a new technology set would be ready for use in production engines.

For fighter engines the ultimate aim was to double the achievable thrust/weight ratio, relative to the F119, to 20:1, while cutting mission fuel consumption by 40 to 50 percent. By 1999, the U.S. Air Force and its contractors had come close to that goal; in particular, General Electric and Allison (which have been teamed in IHPTET since 1994) were due to run an engine in mid-1999 that would meet the fuel consumption goal. A variant of the engine, to run in 2000, will also point the way toward a very-low-observable, agile supersonic-cruise fighter.

The General Electric–Allison approach is a variable-cycle engine. In subsonic cruise, the bypass ratio is increased to lower the jet velocity and increase efficiency; for supersonic flight, all the air is pumped through the core and the pressure and temperature ratio are increased until the engine is almost at stoichiometric conditions—at which all the oxygen inhaled by the engine is combined with fuel—and can produce its theoretical maximum thrust.

One advantage of a variable-cycle engine is that its operation can be controlled over a wide thrust range without adjusting the throat area of the nozzle. Moreover, General Electric and Allison have designed a mechanically fixed thrust-vectoring nozzle using thermal and fluidic techniques, which will be tested during 2000. General Electric refers to the engine as the FENE (fixed exhaust nozzle engine).

This advanced engine will run to Mach 2 and deliver enough thrust for maneuvering flight, without an augmentor, while its higher bypass ratio reduces fuel burn (and infrared emissions) in the cruise. The result is a range improvement of 40 percent in a typical fighter mission. The fixed nozzle is also easy to integrate into a stealthy tailless configuration.

The next step is an IHPTET Phase 3 engine, which includes a more advanced core that has a still higher pressure ratio and fewer stages. It would be made possible by new materials, such as metallic and ceramic composites, which would dramatically reduce the engine's weight.

A Boeing study, produced in 1997 under the U.S. Air Force's Future Aircraft Technology Enhancements (FATE) program, shows the effect of tailless aerodynamics and improved airframe technologies, combined with an advanced fixed-cycle engine with an advanced inlet and mechanically fixed vectored-thrust nozzle. It would carry as much, as far as JSF—a pair of 2,000-pound (900-kilogram) JDAMs and two AIM-9s, more than a 670-nautical mile (1,240-kilometer) interdiction

Successful flight testing of the X-36 has pointed the way toward new-generation tailless fighters with even smaller radar cross-section (RCS) numbers than the F-22. New engine research promises less costly, more stealthy thrust-vectoring technology, combined with substantial improvements in range, while smaller munitions and weapon bays could reduce the fighter's size. JSF, by contrast, is rather conservative in design. Boeing

radius—but would weigh barely half as much.

In early 1999, it is too early to determine the fate of JSF. The writer's best guess is that JSF will neither continue as planned, nor disintegrate completely. Instead, the JSF variants will diverge until they are distinctly different aircraft, but sharing many components and technologies—cousins, not siblings.

The Marines and the Royal Navy are very likely to get their ASTOVL aircraft. It will be slimmed down and should be an acceptable air-combat fighter. If the monster MOB concept gets anywhere, and U.S. forces operate off 3,000-foot-wide floating islands, ASTOVL will come into its own and will probably equip some U.S. Air Force units as well. A later version, with IHPTET technology, could meet the U.S. Air Force and Navy range targets.

The Navy's aircraft, freed from the constraints of the ASTOVL's landing weight, could grow into a long-range strike aircraft with a maximum catapult weight in the 65,000-pound (30,000-kilogram) class and a large internal weapons bay. How soon this aircraft is required will depend on the fortunes of the F/A-18E/F Super Hornet, which is currently looking like the most thoroughly mediocre carrier-based fighter since the Brewster F2A Buffalo.

The Air Force is left with some interesting options. A bomber, like the Navy variant just outlined, makes an interesting alternative to an F-22-based strike aircraft (which could well incorporate JSF technology to reduce its cost). The U.S. Air Force could acquire some of these aircraft, while continuing to buy modernized F-16s to replace some of its older fighters and maintain its force numbers. At the same time, the Air Force could continue to develop advanced technology, with the option of producing a true next-generation fighter around 2015.

The cost of such a program is not as high as one might think. Most of the life-cycle cost of a military aircraft—including development, production, and support—is related to the engine and the avionics. Even if the aircraft are different, many of the projected savings of the JSF program can be gained if the engines, avionics, cockpit, and subsystems use the same parts.

Moreover, even airframes that look different can be closely related. They can use the same materials, including composites and low-observable materials and systems. With computer-controlled machines, airframe parts from different aircraft can be freely mixed on the same production line.

For the Pentagon, this approach has the great advantage of keeping two or more fighter teams together. Ever since the JSF project started, there have been those who doubted that the Pentagon really wanted to set up a fighter monopoly.

Anyone who doubts the practicality of such a production arrangement need only look at Airbus Industrie. The European consortium builds airliners that run from the 100-seat, short-range A318 to the A340-600, which is almost as large as a 747 and has a range of 7,000 nautical miles. All these aircraft use one of two fuselage sections and cab designs. Most of them have near-identical cockpits and the same flight control system. Airbus builds two basic wing designs for most of its aircraft and a modified version of the larger wing for the biggest A340s. Does it save money? Ask Boeing, which has a family of dissimilar aircraft and is finding itself under severe competitive pressure.

Finally, though, one major factor is certain to change the climate in which the key JSF decisions are taken, and another may do so.

U.S. forces are engaged in peace-keeping and enforcement operations throughout the world. If any of them flares up between now and 2001, the outcome could affect military priorities, perhaps favoring carriers, perhaps encouraging investment in special forces or deep-strike weapons rather than JSF.

The factor that will certainly change the climate is the 2000 election. The only sure bet about this process is that it will be a political Passchendaele, from which those who are not killed or maimed will emerge barking mad and dripping with slime. As for its impact on JSF, the only certainty is that no new administration of any political tinge will simply rubber-stamp such a massive project. If a decision is taken before September of 2001, it will be surprising.

An even more radical approach to future air combat operations is the UCAV. Since today's fighters are already highly automated, and may rely on off-board targeting, some experts argue that some missions could be performed by a pilotless weapons platform—smaller, stealthier, and less expensive than a vehicle with a cockpit. The development of a UCAV presents many challenges, but it could appear in time to replace some JSFs. Lockheed Martin

INDEX